VERB

THE ACT OF KNOWING GOD

D.V. ADAMS

All scripture is from the NIV unless otherwise noted.

Italicized scripture passages are used by the author for emphasis.

Quiet Sky Publishing
www.qsky.org

VERB/ ADAMS. -- 1st ed.
ISBN 978-1-7331146-0-8

Cover Design by Patrice at Designery Creative Studio

Dedicated to my Mentor and Friend

TIMOTHY V. JOHNSON

Thank you for decades of friendship
and for showing me what it means
to live a lifestyle of worship

SPECIAL THANKS TO

JESSE CARROLL for allowing me to use some of his
material from his HEARING GOD'S VOICE workshops
(found in chapters Twelve and Thirteen) and for helping me
hear God's voice more clearly.

My editor CALLIE WALKER. Thank you for your advice
and intuitive understanding of this project.
(https://www.proofcorrections.net/)

ONE

Five minutes inside eternity and we will wish that we had sacrificed more, wept more, grieved more, loved and prayed more, and given more.

– Leonard Ravenhill

How we react to life and the array of situations we are daily presented with reflects our true heart and our relationship with God. Our first response to events is a direct reflection of our true self. Here is a great example of those who think they are serving God and the real condition of the heart.

It was rush hour, and a time when emotions can become raw. After following a woman for ten minutes, a policeman turned on his lights pulling the woman over. When the officer arrived at the woman's car, she was agitated and asked if she was speeding.

"No, ma'am you were not speeding."

"Then why did you stop me?"

"Did you put your head out the window and yell obscenities at other drivers?

"Well, yes I did," she said sheepishly.

"Did you use obscene gestures at other drivers?"

Feeling ashamed she said, "Yes, I did. But is that a crime?"

"No, ma'am it's not."

"Then why did you pull me over?"

The officer paused, "Well, ma'am I saw your bumper stickers that say, God is My Co-Pilot, WWJD, and a fish symbol. And well, quite frankly I thought the car was stolen."

Sometimes our view of who we are is not exactly the way our heart reveals us to others. When we start thirsting after God, our mind and heart start the journey of becoming one. It's important to note that thirsting after God is not searching or seeking knowledge; it is longing to be in his presence. The more time you spend with him, the deeper your relationship grows and the greater your desire to be with him becomes.

- God is not a Governor or the President of the United States.
- He isn't the Prime Minister of the United Kingdom or the Pope.
- He isn't an old man with a long white beard sitting on a throne.
- He's your Father.
- He is not distant, hard to approach, or silent.

I am relational. I have a relationship with my wife, my children, my grandchildren, my siblings, my parents, and my friends. God is relational. He desires for you to have a relationship with him.

Muddling through the noise of life can sometimes be distracting. Praying can sometimes be like trying to carry on a conversation with a spouse from across the room while children are yelling and crying in between. It is a daunting task to hear or be heard in times of chaos. But it is during these times God wants you to come to him. The difference is that he is bidding you to move towards his voice to still your heart and mind.

Perhaps talking to God is a difficult, boring task for you. You have tried to pray but it seems your words fall flat on the ground, or you don't receive an answer to your prayer, so you give up.

Maybe you have been hurt by someone, or by people you thought were Christians, or you have painful memories that run deep. You avoid prayer because you feel distant or unworthy.

It may be that you have prayed for many years, but little has happened when you sought God. You *hope* he will answer. You long for his peace and love to fall upon you yet nothing happens. You throw up your hands in frustration and walk away.

God loves you and desperately wants to invite you into his presence. Given the opportunity, he will help, heal, and bless. All you have to do is be willing to spend time with him.

You may become so discouraged that you have no desire to pray. Life can certainly be overwhelming at times and your passion may wane, but your determination should not.

CONVERSATION

We call speech between two people *conversation*. Conversation is a dynamic communication between two individuals.

Both participate in the action. If only one person spoke, it would be a lecture or a monologue, not a conversation. For purposes of clarity, I will call prayer between an individual and God *conversation*, although there is no grammatical difference between conversation and prayer.

How do you approach conversing with God?

Do you do all of the talking?

Do you listen?

Healthy communication begins with mutual respect and honest two–way communication. The candid truth is that often when we communicate with God, we have ulterior motives: needs, desires, and problems; issues other than desiring to be in his presence. There is nothing wrong with offering our needs to God. He knows this and is waiting to act.

But as you wean off the milk of infant Christianity and move on to the meat, your priorities should be changing.

You should be experiencing God.

Desiring him.

Yes, still bringing your needs to him, but longing to be in his presence.

In Luke chapter eleven we find Jesus finishing his conversation with his Father. When he finished, the disciples ask, "Lord, teach us to pray." I don't think they were asking him which words to use; I believe they recognized the intimacy and ease he had while conversing with the Father. They desired to have the same warm, affectionate relationship he had.

I have read and heard others use the term *prayer life* in the context of "How is your prayer life?"

Prayer and life should not be separate terms.

Prayer, or *conversation*, is a lifestyle. It should be a constant, daily habit, or as Brother Lawrence so aptly calls it, *holy habits*. Conversation with God should be as natural as breathing.

VERB

I was discussing with my then eight–year–old son, Aaron, about his day at school. He was (and still is) a straight A student. Trying to boost his confidence I said, "You must be one of the smartest kids in your class."

He paused, then smiled and said, "I don't know if I am one of the smartest, but I'm one of the most pay-attentionables."

I'm not exactly sure what a *pay-attentionable* is, but he was quite content with being one. To have a productive conversation with someone we need to pay attention. It takes a concentrated effort to have an open conversation with someone.

To communicate with God takes energy, real physical energy. Christianity is not an idle lifestyle. In order to pursue God, we must expend energy. It is no different than having a conversation with your best friend. If you care for someone you are interested in what they have to say.

You listen.

The problem I have personally faced and many others have experienced is the feeling of fullness and complacency. Maybe you are experiencing it now:

You are not hungry for God.

You are full.

You are satisfied.

Our activities become habitual and we unknowingly slip into a state of unwitting complacency. The deterioration of a Christian life will not necessarily come from a catastrophe but from complacency. When you lose your passion for God, you stumble into a time that is filled with conflict and loss. You lose sight of what it means to be a child of God who is loved without condition and blessed beyond measure.

Complacency places us between on fire for God and indifferent to him. It causes sin to creep in and make excuses. When we don't want to change or grow in our Christian walk, we become unaware of the wonderful and exciting opportunities God has in store for us. Should we ever be complacent with our Christian life?

Many are.

I was.

Complacency puts us into a lazy, lukewarm lifestyle. Sin has a nasty habit of slinking in and overpowering just enough to keep complacency alive: a quick look at porn, a small fib on taxes, an exaggeration, a white lie, or a general lack of desire to seek God. Soon it can overpower the complacent Christian.

Complacency is the habit you form when you make the conscious decision to stop pursuing God even if it is for a day or an evening filled with prime–time television. It is the lack of will to turn off the TV, computer, or video game and seek God.

Many Christians seek to know more about God but fail to know God.

The opposite of complacency is *passion.*

Passion is an ongoing pursuit to not just know about our Father but by actually getting to know him.

My friend Doug was driving with his five–year–old daughter, Alia, who was snuggled comfortably in the backseat when without warning she began a random prayer: "Dear God, what'cha doin'?"

Innocent and unbridled, this is the relationship God is seeking in all of us. God's heart desires that we speak to him with such simplicity and honesty. As we experience him over and over something in us changes; primarily a deeper understanding of his character and the desire to be with him.

LIFESTYLE CHOICE

Quite often when I came home from work, I was tired. I would turn on the TV and relax. I was complacent. I didn't give God a second thought.

After meeting a few Christians who were actually hearing God and having experiences that I only read about in the Bible, I made a choice that I wanted to experience God, to hear him like they did and like Paul, Peter, Timothy and other New Testament believers did.

I had to change the way I thought of God and the way I was living. A thorough study of what God has to say in Scripture helped me understand that he longs to have a relationship with me. But to have a relationship like New Testament believers comes with a price: *passion* and *discipline*.

If you are not prepared to change your lifestyle then you should close this book and continue the path you are on. However, if you truly desire to have a deep, intimate relationship with God then keep reading.

Conversation with God ushers you from the physical world into the spiritual world. However, many Christians never truly experience the spiritual world because *discipline* and *sacrifice* are involved. How can you converse with God if there is no desire, no passion, no discipline, and no true conviction to your conversation?

When I was beginning my journey into a deeper more intimate relationship with God, I took time to think of him more and tried to listen with more clarity. After everyone had gone to bed, I forced myself to stay up a little longer to worship God and to listen.

It wasn't easy.

At first, I could only do it for about fifteen or twenty minutes.

But I truly wanted to hear his voice clearly.

Soon, I was spending more time worshiping him and experiencing his amazing presence.

Through this I learned (and I am still learning) to seek God for *all* of my decisions. Proverbs 16:9 reminds us, "In their hearts humans plan their course, but the Lord establishes their steps."

Early in this new adventure I was in Missouri on business, staying in the Kansas City area for a week. I had made reservations at a hotel I had never been to before. Instead of asking God where to go, I found an inexpensive hotel that I thought would be perfect for my stay. When I arrived I found the outside of the hotel looking like it did in the pictures. The lobby wasn't updated but not in bad shape. But when I opened the door to my room, I was shocked to find bare wires on the lamps, a very hard bed, and a desk chair that didn't work. It was not a pleasant experience.

So, I had a conversation with God and asked him where I was to go. He told me to go to a certain hotel in a small town.

I obeyed.

When I arrived, I found the hotel to be old and in a sketchy part of town. But I was surprised to find the room comfortable and inviting. However, the laundry area was dimly lit and dank. So, when I had to do my laundry I decided to look around the town for a nicer laundromat and found one on the outskirts of town. It was well lit, had nice machines, and was clean. But when I pulled up to the laundromat, I asked God if this was ok (I made the decision instead of letting God *establish* my steps).

He spoke to me and told me to go back to my hotel room and do my laundry there. So again, I obeyed and went back to my hotel and started my laundry. As I headed back to my room he spoke again and said, "In twenty minutes go back and check your laundry." I waited twenty minutes and went back to the laundry area. When I arrived, I found a man in his early thirties sorting clothes on the floor that he had emptied from a large trash bag. I struck up a conversation with him and asked God what I should say.

He said, "Just listen."

The man introduced himself as Troy and after a few minutes of conversing, he suddenly began pouring his heart out and tears flowed as he told me of the recent death of his father and the current problems he and his wife were experiencing. He was staying at the hotel while he and his wife tried to work out their difference. I was able to pray with Troy and give him some guidance (from God of course).

If I would have established my own steps, I would never have met Troy and had the encounter I did. I had to learn some lessons along the way but conversing with God is an amazing experience. Since that time, I have had many other wonderful adventures with God.

You can have experiences like this too.

Read on.

TWO

To be unknown to God is entirely too much privacy.

– Thomas Merton

We are created as both spiritual and physical. This concept is found in Psalm 84:2 where the Psalmist cries out from his flesh and spirit: "My *soul* yearns, even faints, for the courts of the Lord: my *heart* and my *flesh* cry out for the living God," and Psalm. 103:1, "Praise the Lord, O my soul; all my *inmost* being, praise his holy name" (italics mine).

Today, many Christians are content with knowledge. We are bombarded with so much information every day that we can become desensitized to the simplicity of God's voice. There are many Christians that have intellectual knowledge of spiritual "things" but lack an intimate walk with God. When both your spiritual and your physical being come together, you have intimacy with God.

15

Physically you are calling out to him.

Spiritually you hear him.

CHUCK AND BILL'S GREAT ADVENTURE

In the late 1940s two energetic young evangelists, Chuck and Bill were sent to Europe by a new ministry called Youth For Christ. The evangelistic campaign flamed through Europe and was greater than anyone expected. Upon their return to the States, the support team that followed Chuck and Bill could not stop talking about Chuck. He was an eloquent speaker who easily connected with the crowds.

After returning from Europe, Chuck was in constant demand as an evangelist. It is believed that an average of 150 people were giving their lives to God at each of his crusades. It was reported that in 1953, at a crusade in Evansville, Indiana (population 128,000), over 90,000 citizens came to hear Chuck.[1]

But at the height of his success, Chuck was having doubts about the authenticity of the Bible and crucial

---

1 Retrieved from *http://www.templetons.com/charles/supersales.html*

theological issues. He decided to take a break and pursue further studies at a well–known seminary.

Conversely, during this same time, Bill was growing stronger in his beliefs and refining his skills as an evangelist. His reputation as a skilled orator and passionate evangelist was swelling.

Eventually, Chuck became so despondent with the Bible and Christianity that he left both altogether. He moved back to Canada and started a new career leaving God behind. Later in life, he wrote his biography called: *Farewell to God: My Reasons for Rejecting the Christian Faith.*

The eloquent speaker who packed auditoriums around the world is the late Charles Templeton. Bill went on to become the greatest evangelist of the 20th century. We remember him today as Billy Graham.

Why is it that a man who stood on the precipice of becoming one of history's greatest evangelist gave it all up? Many celebrities like Katy Perry (as a teenager, she recorded a Christian album under the name of Katy Hudson), George Perdikis (the founding member of Newsboys who left the band many years ago and now is a self –proclaimed atheist),

Cee Lo Green (both parents were ordained ministers), Brian Warner (aka Marilyn Manson), and the late Whitney Houston were all given a foundation of Christian principles but left to pursue other passions. The term today is known as *deconversion*.

So, why did Charles Templeton and others who had successful ministries, leave? And why are others leaving the church? Why do people become disillusioned and deconvert?

I pondered this question for many years. I too was seriously contemplating my convictions. Then my life changed forever while I was casually reading the book of Matthew for the umpteenth time. It was in the seventh chapter that I paused and caught my breath: "Not everyone who says to me, 'Lord, Lord,' will enter the kingdom of Heaven, but only he who does the will of my Father who is in Heaven. Many will say to me on that day, 'Lord, Lord, did we not prophesy in your name, and in your name drive out demons and perform many miracles?' Then will I tell them plainly, '*I never knew you.* Away from me you evildoers!'" (Matthew 7:21-23)

Those four key words: *I–never–knew–you.* What?

Know Him? But I am a Christian, I *belong* to Christ. I believe. As the last thought rushed through my head a simple verse came to my mind: James 2:19, "You believe that there is one God...even the demons believe that – and shudder."

Not just believe in God, but to *know* God.

Do you have a fervor and thirst to know God at every opportunity? Are you inspired to turn off your TV and seek God with a passion not out of duty or because the Bible tells you to, but out of desire?

God implores us to give everything to Him. Making an appearance at church and occasionally reading your Bible is not what he longs for. In Revelation 3:15,16 we read, "I know your deeds that you are neither cold or hot. I wish you were one or the other! So, because you are lukewarm–neither hot or cold – I am about to spit you out of my mouth."

God asks us to be hot. The Greek word for hot in this scripture has the meaning of *boiling*. The word for cold has the metaphorical meaning of *sluggish*. So, are you boiling for God or sluggish?

As we read on in chapter three, it continues with Jesus saying, "...be earnest and repent. If anyone *hears* my voice I will come in and eat with him, and he with me. He who has an ear, let him hear."

Are you listening to God or other people? How often do you lend an ear to God that he may speak to you? What do you do with your time?

Watch TV?

Troll the Internet?

Scroll Facebook?

Spending time with God and waiting for his voice takes energy. Loafing in a chair while watching TV, or traveling from one website to another takes very little energy. This is where hot and cold collide and create a lukewarm, sluggish life a life of complacency.

The only way to avoid a lukewarm life and become passionate for God is by spending time with him. Throughout scripture, we are encouraged to walk, follow, listen, and love God with our *whole* heart (Deuteronomy 10:12; Matthew 22:37).

We are surrounded by voices that try to influence us to buy, sell, behave, feel, and do. There is a distinct connection between the voices and noise we hear and the inability to connect with God.

The busier we become, the happier we think we are.

Without conditioning your life to live at a rested pace, you will eventually stop. It may happen in the form of a failed relationship, a death, legal action, or on some other collision course. We are not created to live on adrenaline and feelings alone. Going means we don't have to stop. Stopping means we must deal with emotions, feelings, repressed thoughts, and often pain.

In short, going means don't. Stopping means do.

We have been desensitized to stopping and being still. Our culture nourishes our need to *do*. In stark contrast, God tells us to stop and be calm. You can either react to your pace of life or choose to live within God's schedule. To be quiet means to STOP, and come to a place of rest

Hundreds of books are written on the topic of time management and slowing down. It is not enough to slow down; we must come to a stop and allow ourselves time for God. Kundtz says, "Stopping is doing nothing as much as possible, for a definite period of time...for the purpose of becoming more fully awake and remembering who you are...

The ultimate reason for stopping is going."[2]

Webster defines quiet as *(1) Characterized by an absence or near absence of agitation or activity; (2) Free of noise or uproar; or making little if any sound; (3) Free from disturbance."*

To come to a place of quiet in our hearts means to physically be at rest. Psalm 46:10, "Be still, and know that I am God…" The Hebrew word for *still* is *Raphah* (pronounced raw-faw) which means: "to be quiet, to relax, withdraw, to let drop, abandon, relax, to let go." This verse has two separate statements that have one meaning: *Be still and know.* The Hebrew word for *know* is *Yada* (yaw-dah), which translates: "to know, to perceive, to find out and discern, to *know by experience.*" How can you know God by experience, if you are not still? It is a choice you must make if you truly long to develop a relationship with God.

To walk in worship with God, you must stand in quiet before him. Often God wants you to just be silent. It is in these restrained moments you connect and experience him.

---

2 Kundtz, David. 1998. *Stopping: how to be still when you have to keep going.* Conari Press: Berkeley, CA

Your aspiration should be to allow these moments to draw you closer to him. The more you submit to him the clearer you hear his voice The King James Version says it best in 1 Thessalonians 4:11, "And that ye *study* to be quiet..." You can only know God by experiencing him over and over. To do this, you must first have the attitude of desiring to know and experience him.

YADA Not Yoda

My friend, Kim Hutchcroft plays the saxophone. He doesn't just play for pleasure; he plays for a living as a studio musician. He was one of the founding members of the Grammy–nominated '70s jazz band, *Seawind*, and is now one of the most sought after studio musicians in the world. Kim has appeared with or played on albums with BB King, Michael Jackson, Frank Sinatra, Quincy Jones, Kenny G, Dolly Parton, Michael McDonald, Diana Ross, George Benson, Christopher Cross, and the list goes on and on.

Kim didn't make it to the top of the music industry by practicing the saxophone occasionally. He studied and practiced daily until he reached a level of professional mastery. He knows (yada) his instrument. Practice and experience have made him the best in the business. He still practices daily to continually fine–tune his craft.

Practicing the art of listening requires an act of discipleship; the disciplining of our spiritual lives. It is easier to sit in front of the television and have someone entertain us then to expend energy and quiet our active minds and come into God's glorious presence.

How many times have you watched a program or movie and thought about it for the next few days, or discussed it with others? What you are doing is meditating about the subject matter of the event. God is longing for hearts to come to him with a passion and desire to know him, to meditate on him ,to be in his presence.

It takes minimal physical effort to be entertained. But it takes energy to stay awake and pray or meditate. Psalms 119:147-148 says, "I rise before dawn and cry for help; I have put my hope in your word. My eyes stay open through the watches of the night that I may *meditate* on your promises." Jesus said, "*Watch* and *pray* so that you will not

fall into temptation. The spirit is willing, but the body is weak."
(Matthew 26:41) You won't give into temptation if you are in
constant communion with God.

Why is it that some believe what the Bible says is true,
yet ignore the difficult sayings and skip to the warm fuzzies?

What many Christians fail to realize is the amazing
and incredible experience they could have if they would only
stop, wait, and pray. I compare it to lifting weights: it hurts, it
sometimes aches, and it takes discipline to exercise every day,
but you soon see the results. The muscle must tear down to
build up and become strong. It is in the same manner that you
must tear down your fleshly desires and spend time with God to
become stronger. Dallas Willard says, "A baseball player who
expects to excel in the game without adequate exercise of his
body is no more ridiculous than the Christian who hopes to be
able to act in the manner of Christ when put to the test without
appropriate exercise in godly living."[3]

Thich Nhat Hanh, a Vietnamese–born Buddhist monk,
rallied his countrymen, during the Vietnam War, to aid in
rebuilding villages. He was also an outspoken crusader for

---

3 Willard, Dallas. 1991. *The Spirit of Disciplines: Understanding How God Changes
Lives.* Harper: San Francisco

peace. Because of his activist ways (although peaceful) he was exiled from Vietnam and settled in France. His actions and writings soon garnered the praise and friendship of Martin Luther King and Thomas Merton. In 1967 King nominated Hanh for the Nobel Peace prize.

With ecumenical insight, Hanh writes in, *Living Buddha, Living Christ,* "Discussing God is not the best use of our energy…we touch God not as a concept but as a living reality."[4]

Many Christians believe in God in theory. They are Humanistic–Christians: *Christians whose attitude is to seek, solve, pursue, and maintain life within individual parameters and power, void of faith.*

The true act of worshiping God requires you to come to a place of rest. Not just slowing down to catch the next sermon at church and move on to the next activity, but to stop and wait.

Stopping is not a desirable option in our energized world, but it is a necessity if you truly want to know God.

---

4 Hanh, Thich Nhat. 1995. *Living Buddha, Living Christ.* Riverhead Books: NY

Sometimes Christian living is made complicated, but the cure for common complacency is stopping and acknowledging God.

Learn to hunger after him.

Jesus explains what a worshiper is, "Yet a time is coming and has now come when the true worshipers will worship the Father in spirit and truth, for they are the kind of worshipers the Father seeks." (John 4:23) The real meaning of worship found in the New Testament is found in the Greek word *proskuneo* (pros–koo –neh'–o), which means to *kneel* or *prostrate* before someone. This word is found about sixty times in the New Testament. From this word comes another Greek word, *proskunetes* (pros–koo–nay–tace') which means to fall upon the knees and touch the ground with the forehead as an expression of profound reverence. A true worshipper, therefore, is one who falls down in reverence to God. God is certainly worthy of our respect, admiration, and devotion.

Worship throughout the Bible is often about sacrifice. Romans 12:1 says, "I appeal to you therefore, brothers, by the mercies of God, to present your bodies as a living sacrifice, holy and acceptable to God, which is your spiritual worship."

To offer your bodies is to present yourself to God. It also means to place (your body) at God's disposal (or will) and to bring it into fellowship or intimacy with God. Paul was speaking from the point of someone who didn't separate worship from a lifestyle. Worshiping meant denying sinful desires and finding intimacy with God,

Do you worship God with a *proskunetes* heart?

THREE

Silence is so freaking loud.

– Sarah Dressen

The wind whistled as it grabbed the top layer of snow and violently threw it into the air causing it to fly into powdery dust and disappear. Again, and again it whirled and whistled biting into my cheeks. I pulled my scarf higher onto my nose and pulled my sled another foot up the steep incline to the top of my favorite sledding hill. I was beginning to question my sanity for staying out in this frigid weather.

I was eleven.

I left the house around 10:00 in the morning on the first day of Christmas vacation. My three brothers and two sisters were either sleeping or watching television. I was determined to create some excitement by trekking out into the 200 acres my parents owned in northwestern Michigan. I followed a well–trodden trail and weaved through a grove of trees before I came upon my favorite hill. It was the top of a ridge that opened up into a vast area of sand; a perfect place to fly down the side of the steep hill.

After sledding for about a half an hour, I decided that this would be my last run down the hill. I stepped back, threw the sled down, and jumped on it only to hit a bump just seconds after getting on. I tumbled off and slid half way down the hill. When I finally came to a stop, I rolled over and smacked my hand into the frozen snow in frustration. As I did, I heard the snow crack under the force of my hand. I gathered my sled and started the long cold walk back home.

As I trudged through the snow, I fought the bitter wind by leaning forward with my head down. I listened to the wind as it howled around me. I heard the snow crunch and give way beneath my boots as I labored to make my way home. Just as I reached the trail that would lead me to the house, the wind abruptly stopped blowing. I stopped, stood up straight, turned, and looked behind me. I listened, but heard nothing.

I didn't know at the time what a terrific impact this

would have on me. All I could hear was my heavy breathing. I tried to control it to catch a sound of something. Nothing. Complete silence. I was raised in a large family so it was odd to be surrounded by silence. I was too young to completely process this awesome experience. All I remember thinking is, 'It's nice to be in the quiet.'

WAIT

Tom Brown, Jr. is recognized as the most renowned tracker, wilderness and survival expert in North America. His skills have assisted Police in solving homicide cases and finding forty missing persons. Tom didn't become a gifted tracker overnight. He studied nature and its nuances for many years.

In his book, *The Tracker*, he takes us through his childhood years, growing up with his best friend Rich and learning about survival from an old Apache Indian called Stalking Wolf. Tom and Rich spent every free moment learning how to survive and become a part of nature. Much of what Stalking Wolf taught the boys was to be still and observe.

One day Stalking Wolf asked the boys to feed the birds. A general request that they knew was not as simple as it sounded. They were aware that he had a deeper lesson in store than just feeding the birds. After pondering it for a day, they asked Stalking Wolf how he they should feed the birds.

Stalking Wolf replied, "How would you feed me?"

Tom answered, "I would hand you the food."

Stalking Wolf said, "Go feed the birds." The boys didn't have to ask any questions they knew they were in for an exciting lesson. The next morning they woke up at 4:00 a.m. and headed to the woods. They found a clearing and lay on their backs with arms outstretched, birdseed in each hand.

They waited.

They were quiet.

And they waited some more.

The art of birds eating from your hand is the art of being still. Tom and Rich practiced being still and became masters at it. In the beginning, it was uncomfortable. It was hard to lie on the ground with arms outstretched. It was difficult to learn how to breathe properly. It wasn't easy to control thoughts and urges. But soon it came natural, and birds confidently swooped down, perched on their fingers, and pecked at the birdseed in their hands. Once Tom and Rich changed their attitude and adapted to a different comfort zone, they were able to experience a more rewarding (abundant) life that very few are privileged to enjoy. God wants to bless you abundantly. But you must make yourself available to him.

The discipline needed to achieve an event like Tom and Rich experienced didn't happen all at once. They spent many mornings with no success. But they were determined to experience something new and exciting. To do this, they understood that it would be uncomfortable.

Waiting in conversation is like waiting for birds to eat from your hands. At first it is uncomfortable, maybe even unnatural. Consider Tom, Rich and you:

- They arose early – *You may be tired at night.*
- Their muscles ached – *Your ears may ache from silence.*
- They wanted to move but resisted – *You may want to give up because you're bored.*

- They moved out of their comfort zone – *You find it difficult to make changes.*

Waiting for God is an issue of time and what you do with your mind. It is sometimes difficult to think of time as a positive and rewarding activity. This, I believe, is why Charles Templeton, Katy Perry, and so many others have left God for other passions. It is at this defining moment you either continue in quiet or give up. Like Tom and Rich who were rewarded for waiting, you too will be rewarded for quieting your mind and heart before God. Your reward will be an intimate, life–changing experience if you wait. But many can't get past the discipline of waiting or being still.

If the Bible tells you to do something should you ignore it? Many people do. Most people don't like to wait. It's uncomfortable, and sometimes you may find it boring. But if you truly want a relationship with God, you will wait. The psalmist encourages us to wait:

- "In the morning, Lord, you hear my voice; in the morning I lay my requests before you and wait expectantly." (Psalms 5:3)

- Wait for the Lord; be strong and take heart and wait for the Lord." (Psalms 27:14)

- "Be still before the Lord and wait patiently for him…" (Psalms 37:7)

- "I wait for the Lord, my whole being waits, and in his word, I put my hope." (Psalms 130:5)

The art of listening and waiting have become lost in the busyness of our culture. In his timely book, *CrazyBusy,* Dr. Edward Hallowell says that "…lingering is a lost art. Such is our hurry and our need for constant stimulation that a modern romantic conversation might go like this:

"I love you."

"Oh good, now what's your next point?"

"…if we're not careful, we'll get so busy that we will miss taking the time to think and feel."[1]

---

1 Hallowell, Edward. 2006. *Crazybusy.* Ballantine Books: NY

How many times have you heard someone say, *"Been keeping busy?"* or something to that effect? While teaching a college course on Personal Development, I asked my students what was the first thing they did after they got into their car. The overwhelming response was, "Turn the music on." Almost every student complained that they couldn't stand the silence. They thrived on noise.

For a class project, I had them spend two hours alone and write a paper about their experience. The outcome was just what I expected. It wasn't a problem finding the time; it was a mental challenge to deal with their inner self. Most of the students struggled with facing their thoughts, their hurts, and in short, who they were.

Many Christians are no different; they don't like to approach solitude and know if they do they must deal with themselves. The author of Lamentations has this to say about being silent before God: "The Lord is good to those whose hope is in him, to the one who seeks him; it is good to *wait quietly* for the salvation of the Lord. It is good for a man to bear the yoke while he is young. Let him sit alone in silence, for the Lord has laid it on him" (Lamentations 3:25-28). The problem is that many don't know how to be still long enough to hear God's voice.

Being in a quiet environment gives us the time to wash the dust from the day and soak in God's presence. The more you practice doing this, the more it will linger with you throughout the day, throughout the week, and soon you are longing for him more and more.

BE STILL AND KNOW

Children have a difficult time standing still. The curiosity of life around them is too enticing to stop and be still. When it involves spending time alone with God, adults are not much different. You can become enamored with life around you instead of knowing the one you invited inside.

The act of quiet comes from a lifestyle of discipline. To be a disciple is to refrain from certain gratifications made available by worldly pleasures. In Isaiah 30:15 God calls to us to be quiet, "In repentance and rest is your salvation, in *quietness* and trust is your strength." The Hebrew word for *repentance* has the meaning of *withdrawing* or *retirement*. In other words 'stop what you have been doing and be quiet so I can speak and you can hear.'

Most writers on the thoughts of solitude and the steps to a deeper relationship with God call us to take action, to discipline our lives to know God better:

- Brother Lawrence uses the term, "mortify your senses." [2]

- Thomas à Kempis cries out that we must, "lay the ax to the root [of sin]". [3]

- Thomas Merton warns, "Keep your eyes clean and your ears quiet and your mind serene."[4]

- Teresa of Avila counsels, "We can only learn to know ourselves and do what we can namely, surrender our will and fulfill God's will in us."[5]

The simple of act of denying yourself TV time in exchange for prayer is an act of discipline. Fasting is simply

---

2 Brother Lawrence. 1982. *The Practice of The Presence of God.* Whitaker House: Springdale, PA
3 à Kempis, Thomas. 1952. *The Inner Life.* Penguin Books: NY
4 Merton, Thomas. 1961. *New Seeds of Contemplation.* New Directions Books: NY
5 Teresa, of Avila. 1991. *The Way of Perfection.* Doubleday: NY

denying the worldly pleasures for the benefit of spiritual gain. How do you expect to live forever with God and rest in the luxury of his amazing love and presence without getting to know him now? The busier you become the more you need to be still.

WORD OR WORD?

How do you define *faith*? Most people will quickly quote Hebrews 11:1 "Now faith is confidence in what we hope for and assurance about what we do not see." Or Matthew 17:20 (ESV), "Because you have so little faith. Truly, I tell you, if you have faith as small as a mustard seed, you can say to this mountain, 'Move from here to there,' and it will move. Nothing will be impossible for you."

These are wonderful definitions. But let's take a step backwards. Where does faith come from? How do you grow in faith? Roman's 10:17 says, "So then faith comes by hearing, and hearing by the *word* of God" (NKJV). The Greek definition of *word* pronounced *rhema* (ray-mah) is: *that which is or has been uttered by the living voice, thing spoken, any sound produced by the voice and having definite meaning.* The Bible is called God's *word* and without a doubt it is. However, in

Romans, Paul conveys the meaning of listening to God's present voice. This Greek word *rhema*, is also found in the following verses:

- Matthew 4:4, "But He answered and said, "It is written, 'Man shall not live by bread alone, but by every *word* that proceeds from the mouth of God." (NKJV). The New Century Version translates this verse: "Jesus answered, 'It is written in the Scriptures, 'A person does not live by eating only bread, but by everything God *says.*'"

- Ephesians 6:17, "Take the helmet of salvation, and the sword of the Spirit, which is the *word* of God..."

- 1 Peter 1:25, "...but the *word* of the Lord stands forever..."

The Bible is our standard, our handbook for living a victorious Christian life, but it not to be a substitute for listening to God's voice. To listen means, you must hear the voice speaking to you. You learn to read by reading and listening to the person teaching you to read. That is how you process learning. You converse by conversing and listening to God; this is how intimacy is born.

THE REAL LIFE

Jesus said, "It is written: 'Man shall not live on bread alone, but on every word that comes from the mouth of God.'" (Matthew 4:4). The word for live found here is from the Greek *zao* (dzah'-o) which means: *to live, breathe, to enjoy life, to be full in vigor, to be fresh, strong, and efficient.* It is the same word found in John 10:10 "The thief comes only to steal and kill and destroy; I have come that they may have *life*, and have it to the full." The Message Bible translates it, "A thief is only there to steal and kill and destroy. I came so they can have real and eternal life, more and better life than they ever dreamed of."

How can you have a *real* and an *eternal* life if you don't listen to what God is saying? Yes, God can speak to you in many different ways. But, fleeces and cryptic messages need to wane, as you grow closer to Him.

When you think of Gideon what do you think of?

Most people associate Gideon with his fleeces asking God to prove that he really was asking him to deliver the Israelites from the Midianites. He lay the fleece on dry arid ground and told God that if it was wet in the morning, he would know it was a true valid command from God.

Many people take this story and rationalize it to mean that they too can use something to ask God to act. This isn't necessarily wrong but that's not what this story represents. Gideon was a military man and he knew the risk involved if he went against the Midianites. Even after experiencing an angel who made fire appear from a rock, and experiencing God cause dry wool on very dry ground become wet, he still would not obey and asked for one more miracle.

But some fail to remember that he had an ongoing conversation with God. In Judges 6:12 (and following) an angel – a messenger of God – first speaks to Gideon. But in verse 14 God speaks directly to Gideon:

When the angel of the Lord appeared to Gideon, he said, "The Lord is with you, mighty warrior."

"Pardon me, my lord," Gideon replied, "but if the Lord is with us, why has all this happened to us? Where are all his wonders that our ancestors told us about when they said, 'Did

not the Lord bring us up out of Egypt?' But now the Lord has abandoned us and given us into the hand of Midian."

The Lord turned to him and said, "Go in the strength you have and save Israel out of Midian's hand. Am I not sending you?"

"Pardon me, my lord," Gideon replied, "but how can I save Israel? My clan is the weakest in Manasseh, and I am the least in my family."

The Lord answered, "I will be with you, and you will strike down all the Midianites, leaving none alive."

In the next few verses, God and Gideon continue to communicate back and forth. I am not opposed to fleeces or knowing that God can speak in many different ways. But hearing God's voice is much more exciting and rewarding.

Be still.

Listen, and see what happens.

FOUR

Are you content with constantly having secondhand revelation of truth, and only hearing from God through others? Or will you pay a price to hear God as a way of life?

– Joy Dawson

Some people have a tendency to want someone else to talk to God for us. They prefer the shortcut: *instant gratification.* Biblical history has shown us a scramble to have a medium, prophet, priest or other mediator speak on behalf of the so–called Believer.

Have things changed since the advent of prophets and priests? I know of Christians who seek psychics to interpret their life situation. Many Christians look for signs in sermons or advice from others *instead* of seeking God. The lack of hunger for God preempts the experience of being in his presence.

The Bible tells us to *listen.* Remember Revelation 3:20 "Here I am! I stand at the door and knock. If anyone *hears* my voice and opens the door, I will come in and eat with him, and he with me."

You can have a radical and exciting life with God if you listen.

DE–MYSTIFYING THE MYSTICS

The word Saint appears in the Bible over ninety times. In the New Testament, the word *hagios* (hag'-ee-os) is the same word used for *Saint* and *Holy* as in the *Holy* Ghost. The word mystic or mysticism does not occur in the Bible at all. It wasn't until the mid 14th Century that it was used.

Today, we call great men and women of God who lived their lives in a holy manner: *mystics* or *Christian mystics.* Brother Lawrence, Julian of Norwich, George Fox, Theresa of Avila, Madame Guyon, St. John of the Cross, and A.W. Tozer are a few of the men and women associated with Christian mysticism.

For many modern Christians, the word mysticism may conjure up visions of Tibetan monks sitting cross–legged

on the edge of a mountain chanting "Omm, Omm, Omm."
We often attribute mysticism to Eastern religions such as
Buddhism, Hinduism, Sufism, and the like. However, the
meaning of mysticism or a mystic is *one who aspires to
connect with God or higher power,* and was first used to
reference men and women who had a deeper understanding of
God than those of their day.

The Merriam–Webster defines mysticism as "the belief
that direct knowledge of God, spiritual truth, or ultimate
reality can be attained through subjective experience (as
intuition or insight)."

The Cambridge Dictionary interprets it more directly:
"the belief that there is hidden meaning in life or that each
human being can unite with God."

And the Compact Oxford English Dictionary defines
a mystic as "a person who seeks by contemplation and self-
surrender to attain unity with the Deity and reach truths
beyond human understanding."

Quaker author Rufus Jones notes that, "Mystical
Devotion means direct, firsthand fellowship with God, and
the deepened life–results which emerge...the emphasis on

immediate awareness of relations with God, on a direct and intimate consciousness of the Divine Presence. It is religion in its most acute, intense and living stage."

If you are seeking God and learning to know him, you are a mystic. Jon Zuck explains Christian mysticism this way:

"To know God directly shows that mysticism is different from any passive or legalistic kind of Christianity. It means:

- That while you honor the Scripture, you want to know God directly, not just through Scripture.

- While you respect your heritage of teachings about God, you want to know God directly, not through doctrines and teachings.

- While you gather in communal worship, you want to know God directly, not just through the Church."[1]

---

1 Retrieved from *http://www.frimmin.com/faith/mysticismintro.html*.
Used with permission.

Mysticism is simply being a Christian that connects with God. It is not a spiritual mystery to be labeled a *mystic*. It is only a word. However, the action behind what this word defines is the difference between one who connects with God (knows Him), and one who does not have a relationship with him but who believes in Him in theory (Humanistic–Christian).

You are either a Humanistic–Christian or a Proskunetes Believer. You are either aspiring to know God (Matt. 7:21-23), or you are not. How can you say that you are a child of God (John 1:12) if you aren't getting to know your Father? How can you declare that Jesus lives within you (Galatians 2:20) if you only believe it in theory?

The saints of Scripture and the Christian mystics of old were one in the same. The early believers didn't need another word for who they were and how they were to live. They understood without question. They knew that by knowing God, it would allow them to bring the spiritual world into the natural world.

PRACTICING GOD'S PRESENCE

Brother Lawrence, a Carmelite layman during the 1600's, was a lowly kitchen worker of the Discalced Carmelite in Paris. His uncanny approach to developing an intimate relationship with God is chronicled in *The Practice of the Presence of God*. Brother Lawrence found an incredible time of worship while just washing dishes. It may be hard to fathom someone standing at a large sink, scraping off plates of half-eaten meals and worshiping God unrestrained but such was Brother Lawrence.

At first, he despised his job as a lowly kitchen worker. But, he began to realize that God was alive in everything he did, no matter how frivolous or humbling it may be. He found a moment–to–moment, second–to–second encounter with God. In the midst of dirt, grime, chaos, and humbling labor, he discovered what it meant to experience God.

It is in the familiar routine of life that God lives. Foster say, "The discovery of God lies in the daily and the ordinary, not in the spectacular and heroic. If you cannot find God in the routines of home and shop, then you will not find him at all."

LISTENING

Listening means you cease talking.

Kahlil Gibran takes notice and says, "You talk when you cease to be at peace with your thoughts…And when you can no longer dwell in the solitude of your heart you live in your lips, and sound is a diversion and a pastime…There are those among you who seek the talkative through fear of being alone."[2]

Instead of dwelling in solitude, some would rather dwell in noise. If Gibran were alive today, he might revise his thoughts and say, "There are those among you who seek the Internet, music, chatter, gossip, and other noise, for fear of being alone." To listen means, you must focus our thoughts on the one you are listening to. When your focus is diluted with other noises or thoughts it is difficult to hear God conversing with you.

To listen takes energy.

The lack of listening causes laziness in your spirit, which in turn quenches our ability to hear from God. Even

---

2 Gibran, Kahlil. 1923. *The Prophet.* Alfred A. Knopf: NY

in the distractions of a busy monastery kitchen Brother Lawrence found solitude in his heart. He says, "For me, the time of action does not differ from the time of prayer, and in the noise and clatter of my kitchen, while several persons are together calling or as many different things, I possess God in as great tranquility as when upon my knees..."

What would happen if you found the tranquility of God in everything you did?

Revival would explode in your world.

If God speaks once about a particular subject in the Bible should you take notice? Does it concern you that he is trying to get your attention? What if he speaks ten times about this subject? Would you begin to think this is something to seriously consider? Now, what if he speaks twenty times? Is it time to make a change in your life because now it has become a theme with him? God speaks about listening over 90 times in the Bible. In the KJV "...thus saith the Lord..." appears over 400 times.

If you say you obey God and want to do what he asks of you, are you listening?

I recently read Joy Dawson's wonderful book, *Forever*

Ruined For The Ordinary. I love her quote I used at the beginning of this chapter especially when she challenges us with "...*will you pay a price to hear God as a way of life.*"

What does it mean to you to pay a price?

FIVE

In our stillness, we acknowledge God's greatness, and
we are at peace in our life. Stillness saturates us
in the Presence of God.

– E'yen A. Gardner

I consider my former pastor a mystic (and saint). The late Charles Hawkins, a humble yet devoted pastor, taught his flock to get on their knees (literally) and seek God. I vividly remember as a child, the entire congregation of our small country church kneeling down at our wooden pews and just conversing. Charles often deviated from his Sunday sermon and taught us to converse with our Father.

TWO MEN ON A PLATFORM

One of my favorite stories is about two men on a stage in a crowded auditorium with standing room only. The first, a handsome, well–dressed young man, rose from his seat and briskly walked to the podium. "The Lord is my Shepherd…" he began with the eloquence of a great orator, "I shall not want…" When he finished the Twenty–third Psalm the crowd leaped to their feet and began cheering and clapping. Never before had they heard such a beautiful prayer.

After a few minutes of applause and kudos to the young man, the crowd settled down. The second, a commonly dressed elderly man, pulled himself up with his cane and hobbled to the podium. "The Lord is my Shepherd…" he began; his voice, rough and sometimes crackling. It was evident he was not a skilled speaker as the young man was. When he finished, he turned and slowly walked back to his seat. The crowd didn't cheer. They didn't even applaud. But something strange began to happen. Some people were crying, some praying, some sitting stunned. After a few brief moments, the young man walked to the podium and said, "Ladies and gentlemen. I would like to explain what has happened here. You see, I know the Twenty–third Psalm, but my friend here…he knows the Shepherd."

Do you *know* the Shepherd?

Do you have an ongoing, intimate relationship with him?

Are you hungry to be filled with his love, his grace, his mercy, and to know his voice? Listen to the words Jesus says in John 10:27-28, "My sheep *listen* to my voice; I *know* them, and they follow me." He doesn't stop with this declaration, he adds, "I give them eternal life, and they shall never perish."

Would you get married and never try to get to know your spouse? What if all you did was listen to what other people had to say about your spouse? It would be absurd to think a relationship would ever grow or be healthy. A positive relationship is one where communication is open, honest, and two–way.

FLEETING MOTIONS OF AFFECTION

I recently read a book by a woman who is one of the few women fully authorized as a Buddhist Zen master. She shared how she retreated to a secluded cabin for a few weeks to find release from her frustration and anxieties through daily rituals of disciplined meditation.

As I meditated on her retreat in the woods I soon realized that she did experience some positives from her retreat: she eagerly disciplined herself to increase her bowing time, she fought to control her desire for food and other fleshly cravings, and she had a heightened awareness of ordinary chores. Yet, she didn't have a connection to anything except herself and her surroundings.

In stark contrast to the female Zen master, my friend Grammy Nominee, Dove Award winner, author, and humanitarian, Margaret Becker shared her retreat experience in her book, *Coming Up For Air.* Here we find Margaret seeking to find peace in her life by retreating to a house on a peaceful beach in Florida. We follow her journey as she comes to terms with herself and her relationship with her heavenly Father. Margaret and the female Zen master both struggled in the same way to find peace in the chaos of their lives. However, the striking difference is that, although the female Zen master was able to lower her blood pressure and become more disciplined, she didn't relate to anything except herself.

Margaret's experience was radically different. She

writes, "My life came to a crossroads. Propelled by a busy schedule that spiraled until it allowed little time for things that mattered, I made a radical choice. I stopped. I waited. I tried to listen, and eventually, I heard. I changed. I re-prioritized. The result was a deep and significant awakening that impacted my life and altered my future direction. Since this very personal encounter with God, my life has not been the same." [1]

Brother Lawrence echoes her sentiments, "It is not enough to know God as theory, from what we read in books, or feel some *fleeting motions of affection* for Him, brief as the wave of feeling, or glimpse of the Divine...our faith must be alive, and we must make it so, and by means lift ourselves beyond all these passing emotions to worship the Father and Jesus Christ in all their divine perfection..."[2] (italics added)

Margaret found a connection. She struggled, she hurt, and she was uncomfortable. Yet she stood steadfast, sometimes in silence. She moved beyond the fleeting motions

---

1 Becker, Margaret. 2006. *Coming Up for Air: Simple Acts to Redefine Your Life*
   NavPress: CO
2 Brother Lawrence.

of affection and discovered a deep, rich, life–changing relationship with God. She took the time to know her Shepherd.

DISTURBANCES

The best situation for tracking an animal is having ideal weather with ideal conditions. But for Tom Brown Jr., (The Tracker) this was rarely the case. Most of the time the track was a few days old, or rain or snow had disturbed the track. However, it was not impossible to follow the trail even if snow, rain, or wind caused a disturbance in the ideal situation.

Tom would crouch down and carefully examine the track, and look for anything that would reveal the true nature of the animal, or where the animal was going. He inspected every inch of the track looking at how the wind settled the dirt, or how deep the track was at the particular time he discovered it. After carefully scrutinizing every aspect of the track he made his conclusions. He didn't hurry on (a Humanistic–Christian trait) wondering how much time he would lose if he stopped. He knew he would be better equipped to know which way to go if he took the time to stop and examine the disturbance.

Tom's actions were to stop and observe. Your actions should be to stop and allow God to work. As you converse with him about the disturbance in our life, you need to examine what he can teach you from it. But, how many times do you tend to hurry to fix a disturbance in our life instead of waiting?

Has life thrown you a curve ball and you are left dealing with unexpected problems? Whether it is finances, marriage, children, or work, it can seriously disturb your relationship with God. When dealing with pressures and stress, you are faced with an option: (1) you can be a Humanistic–Christian and try to solve the problem within your own means, or (2) you can to continue to seek God.

What is your first response to a problem?

Many Christians are too busy with Humanistic–Christian beliefs to understand that God is calling them to stop and listen. They believe they can do a better job of caring for their lives than God can.

I was once given counsel by an elderly Christian lady

who suggested that I *"put feet to my prayers."* She believed that we needed to help God solve our problems. She didn't understand the command by God (Psalms 46:10) to wait in prayer and have faith that he will, in his way, take care of our disturbances.

Waiting and being quiet before God, is an act of faith, an act of our spiritual worship (Romans 12:1). What a tremendous opportunity God gives us to get to know him better. Life may at times be difficult, but the next time you are going through a *life–disturbance* moment remember that God is waiting to have a conversation with you. Going to him for your problem should be your first response. We live in an ordinary world, but through intimate experiences with God, life becomes extraordinary.

Do you want to have extraordinary experiences with God?

SIX

The mind, if overly active, may affect and disturb the quietness of the spirit.

– Watchman Nee

My younger brother John is a mechanical genius. He can fix almost anything. He continually amazes me with his insight into mechanics and construction. For over thirty years he worked at a milk–processing plant. While working in the maintenance department, he was called out of bed in the middle of the night to help with a machine that had stopped working which brought the entire production process to a screeching halt. John knew every machine in the plant (*yada*) and was well acquainted with the way they worked.

The operators and supervisors explained to John that the machine jammed, but after they un–jammed it they were unable to restart it. Before calling John, they spent two hours trying to figure out the problem with no avail.

John slowly walked around the machine, examined it closely, then stood back with the supervisors and other workers and studied it. After pondering the situation, John turned to the operator and asked if he had pushed the restart button. Much to his embarrassment, he shyly answered, "No." He pushed the button, and the machine came to life. John knew the problem because he took the time to examine the situation, and he spent time getting to know the machines. But he didn't hurry.

Sometimes disturbances in your life can be more complicated than they really are. When in reality all you need to do is seek, wait, and sometimes just push the reset button, which is to stop, be quiet, and listen.

KNOW ME

If someone were to ask you what God has been directly speaking to you about, what would you answer?

Could you answer?

Hebrews 3:15 declares "Today, if you hear his voice, do not harden your hearts…" and God commands us to listen to Him, as found in Isaiah 28:23, "Listen and hear my voice; pay attention and hear what I say." You can only hear when you *stop* to listen.

One of the reasons God calls you to still your life even during terrible disturbances, is to help you get to know Him. How do you expect to live forever with God and rest in the luxury of his amazing love and presence without getting to know him now?

God desires to have a relationship with you, but many are unwilling to spend time getting to know him. Immediately after he makes this stirring statement in Matthew 7:21-23, Jesus immediately follows (in verses 24–27) with, "Therefore everyone who hears these words of mine and puts them into practice is like a wise man who built his house on the rock. The rain came down, the streams rose, and the winds blew and beat against that house, yet it did not fall, because it had its foundation on the rock. But everyone who hears these words of mine and does not put them into practice is like a foolish man who built his house on sand. The rain came down, the streams rose, and the winds blew and beat against that house, and it fell with a great crash."

So, what does it mean to put God's spoken word (*rhema*) into practice?

Your foundation is built on how strong your relationship with God is. Sadly, many Christians won't spend time alone with God. They unknowingly build their foundation on sand. What is also interesting about this passage of scripture is the word he uses for foolish. He could have used the word, *aphfron* (af–ron) which means foolish, stupid, or to act rashly. Instead, Jesus uses the word, *moros* (mo–ros) which has the meaning of being godless. He is describing two types of people: those that know him, and those that say they know him in theory; those that play, and those who sit on the sidelines.

None of us want to say that we are godless, that's absurd. However, in theory, many believe in God, but are too busy to develop an intimate relationship with him.

Søren Kierkegaard utters these strong words of caution, "The apostasy from Christianity will not come about openly by everybody renouncing Christianity; no, but slyly, cunningly, knavishly, by everybody assuming the name of being Christian, thinking that in this way all were most securely secured against . . . Christianity, the Christianity of the New Testament, which people are afraid of, and therefore industrial priests have invented under the name of Christianity a sweetmeat which has a delicious taste, for which men hand out money with delight." [1]

If you discipline yourself to spiritual training, you will be just like the wise man who, took his time (found contentment in listening to God), labored hard (disciplined his life by getting before God instead of his TV), and was able to resist the storm (temptation). He, therefore, lived a wonderful, Jesus–centered life because he took the time to know God.

If you don't stop to know him, you are like the foolish man, the godless man, the one who doesn't have a relationship with God. I don't want to be like the foolish man who isn't able to be in God's presence because he didn't take the time to develop a relationship with his heavenly Father.

I find it curious that Jesus didn't say the wise man built his house on solid ground, instead said he built it on rock. The word he uses is *petra*, which means a rock or rocky ground.

---

1 Lowrie, Walter. 1942. *Kierkegaard's Attack Upon Christendom.* Princeton University Press: Princeton, NJ

He could have used the word ge (*ghay*) for ground, as found in the following KJV verses:

- "But he that received seed into the good ground (*ge*) is he that heareth the word, and understandeth [it]; which also beareth fruit, and bringeth forth, some an hundredfold, some sixty, some thirty" (Matthew 13:23).

- "Verily, verily, I say unto you, except a corn of wheat fall into the ground (*ge*) and die, it abideth alone: but if it die, it bringeth forth much fruit" (John 12:24).

- "Then said the Lord to him, Put off thy shoes from thy feet: for the place where thou standest is holy ground (*ge*)" (Acts 7:33).

Doesn't that seem odd? Why would he use the word *petra* which means *rock* instead of the word *ground*? You need to drill down deep into the rock to get a strong hold on the foundation. I used to work in construction, and I don't know any contractor who would love to build on rocky terrain. A smooth solid site is always ideal. Building a house on rock takes more time to build than a house built on sand.

The Christian whose strong house is built on rock is the one who spends time with the Chief Contractor and is given instruction on how to complete the project. There are almost 100 instances of God's voice speaking to man throughout Scripture. If God didn't want to speak to us, we would all be puppets on a string with no will or desire for him. But God desires to have a relationship with you.

Is your true desire to have a relationship with him?

SEVEN

Never miss a good chance to shut up.

– Will Rogers

Classic children's stories can often have deep spiritual connotations. For example, consider the story of the Three Little Pigs:

- The first pig builds his house out of straw. He believes it is strong enough to keep out the big, bad wolf. Sadly, he is mistaken.
- The second pig is a tad smarter and builds his house out of sticks; a little stronger than straw, but not strong enough to keep the wolf out.
- The third little pig decides to take his time and do it right. He builds his house out of bricks and it

withstands the mighty wind of the wily wolf.

Where are you at in your relationship with God? Are you building your relationship out of straw, by thinking that going to church is enough, or socializing with other Christians and giving them the impression that you have it all together?

Are you building your relationship with sticks? You toss up some prayers to God, maybe daily, but it's a one-sided relationship. You talk but don't give God the time of day. You religiously do your daily devotions, but you don't devote your whole being to God. You give him the ten or twenty minutes a day you think he deserves. Yes, that is more than building a relationship out of straw. But are you growing closer to God? Do you know what his will is for you?

The third little pig took time to make his house strong, just as the wise man did. God desires us and wants us to have a relationship with him. Many Christians are afraid to step out in faith. They take on a Humanistic–Christian mindset. They believe that although God exists, life–disturbances will be handled better if they take charge. To those that have this attitude, they believe faith is a large obstacle that is reserved for people who have time to be silent and pray.

ALONE WITH GOD

Recognize that the value in pausing and saying nothing is far more pleasing to God than service or busyness; this is the only way you can contemplate and converse with him.

Contemplation is the focus, the concentration on spiritual things as a form of private devotion, a state of mystical awareness of God's being; an act of considering with attention. And the key to contemplation is

Listening.

Waiting.

Being available.

The word *contemplation*, is often used in the same context with prayer or meditation. However, contemplation means to *separate something from its environment*. So, does this mean that during a hectic day or the rise of unexpected trials, you have to search out and try to find a quiet place to go through a mind–numbing time of meditation? In the context of contemplation of God, it means to *spiritually* separate yourself from the worldly environment. I recently saw a bumper sticker that said: MY CAR IS MY PRAYER CLOSET. If someone cannot find time for God, they are too busy, and their priorities are not in order.

HEAVENLY WORSHIP

Do you think of Heaven? How often? Heaven is our future home. If you are unable to devote your life to worshiping, experiencing, and loving God now, what do you think your relationship with him will be like when you live with him forever if you don't know him now?

What can you learn from living with him in heaven? A close look at the Old and New Testament opens a window into what you can look forward to when you see God face to face:

You discover heavenly worship. In the Old Testament, Nehemiah shares with us that the multitudes of Heaven worship God, "You alone are the LORD. You made the heavens, even the highest heavens, and all their starry host, the earth and all that is on it, the seas and all that is in them. You give life to everything, and the multitudes of heaven worship you." (Nehemiah 9:6).

You find heavenly beings praising God. In Isaiah, we read of his vision as he sees, "...the Lord seated on a throne, high and exalted, the train of his robe filled the temple. Above him were seraphs, each with six wings: With two wings they covered their faces, with two they covered their feet, and with two they were flying. And they were calling to one another: 'Holy, holy, holy is the Lord Almighty; the whole earth is full of his glory.'" (Isaiah 6:1-3).

You discover humility. The book of Revelation gives us another view of what heavenly worship will look like. In Chapter four we see twenty-four Elders falling down, crying out to God, "You are worthy, our lord and God, to receive glory and honor and power, for you created all things, and by your will, they were created and have their being" (Revelations 4:10-11). In verses 11:16, 17 we discover they each have a seat that surrounds the throne of God. The Elders, persons of honor, leave their seats of prestige, stand up, cry out a declaration, and fall (*proskunetes*) in humble submission before God. They not only lie down and prostrate themselves, but they first throw their gold crowns at the feet of God. The word for throw or cast is the Greek word *ballo* (bal'-lo), which has the meaning of throwing something without caring where it falls, and to give over to one's care uncertain about the result.

A modern example of this incredible act of worship by the Elders might be the same as a wealthy man taking his wealth and giving it all away offering himself to God, without a second thought to his intentions. The Elders gave their most prized possessions without question and fell prostrate in loving reverence and honor to Him. The heart of a God–centered lifestyle conversation begins with the attitude of complete surrender to God.

Would it seem unbelievable to go to church on Sunday morning and see your leaders falling prostrate? And for the congregation to spend the entire morning just giving praise to God? This is what is happening in heaven. If you are unwilling to kneel, cry, shout, and sing to God now how will you be ready to do it when you meet him in Heaven?

These are the activities of Heaven. Our 24/7, dimensional understanding makes it somewhat difficult to grasp the full magnitude of what is happening here. To have conversation with God, you must first make the conscious decision to make changes in your life. You should always be striving to draw closer to God. But to know God means you must listen, wait, converse, and act accordingly. It only occurs when a change in your lifestyle, your current way of processing life is put into consistent practice.

In our hectic culture, it's sometimes very difficult to find time to stop and contemplate God. The conundrum here is: do you want to seek after God or do you want to continue your current lifestyle?

Indian peace activist Mahatma Gandhi was jailed on numerous occasions. He spent over 2000 days in jail, which translates to nearly six years, most of which was in solitary confinement. Gandhi used his time in solitude to clear his mind, to contemplate, to meditate, and focus on the issues that mattered most in his life. The rest is history.

The act of contemplation is an act of obedience, an act of discipline. In the New Testament we find Jesus, and his disciples, often getting away from the hustle and bustle to find a quiet place to devote more of their time to God (Mark 6:30-31). Jesus understood the need to continually grow closer to his Father through times of solitude. Being alone is a therapeutic, healing time with our Father.

If Jesus did it, why aren't you doing it?

SOLITUDE AND PSYCHOLOGY

Solitude is no longer a closet topic. Psychologists are discovering that solitude is an effective healing tool. The late Dr. Ester Buchholz, former Director of the Steinhardt's School Psychology Program at New York University, spent much of her career exploring the role of solitude as a curative aid for various disorders. Here are some tidbits of her thoughts on solitude from her book, *The Call of Solitude*, published in *Psychology Today*:

"Meaningful alone time, it turns out, is a powerful need and a necessary tonic in today's rapid-fire world. Indeed, solitude allows us to connect to others in a far richer way..." (On Religion) "...religion no longer provides a place for quiet retreat but instead offers "mega churches" of social and secular amusement...Religion must provide time for prayer and meditation. And the relationship of the individual to God is one solution to the paradox of aloneness and relatedness. For religion to have its greatest appeal, it must allow time for solitude..." [1]

The majority of focus in the field of psychology is the social interaction between people and how they relate to each other. However, a new and growing trend is research in the area of solitude. Clinicians and researchers are discovering solitude as a curative aid. Psychology Today editor, Hara Estroff Marano, said,

"As the world spins faster and faster -- or maybe it just seems that way when an email can travel around the world in fractions of a second -- we mortals need a variety of ways to cope with the resulting pressures. We need to maintain some semblance of balance and some sense that we are steering the ship of our life. Otherwise, we feel overloaded, overreact to minor annoyances, and feel like we can never catch up. As far as I'm concerned, one of the best ways is by seeking, and enjoying, solitude...Solitude suggests peacefulness stemming from a state of inner richness.

1 Bucholz, Ester. 1997. *The Call of Solitude: How spending time alone can enhance intimacy.* Simon and Schuster: NY. Psychology Today. Publication Date: Jan/Feb 1998

It is a means of enjoying the quiet and whatever it brings, that is satisfying and from which we draw sustenance. It is something we cultivate. Solitude is refreshing; an opportunity to renew ourselves. In other words, it replenishes us..."[2]

To better prepare yourself for eternity with God, you must first learn to discipline your life. When you practice being quiet, an act of discipline, you learn to listen. Silence is the internal dialogue God uses to speak to us.

Often conversation (prayer) as a one-sided relationship. God is desirous to speak and teach you. You only need to be willing.

Richard Foster succinctly puts it this way, "Do we really think we can experience integration of heart and mind and spirit with an erratic prayer life? Do we really believe we can, like Moses, "speak face to face" with God as someone would a friend by our unpredictable prayers? No, we develop

---

2 Marano, Hara Estroff. *What is Solitude?*. Psychology Today Magazine.
  25 August 2003

intimacy by regular association."[3]

Regular association is the act of continually being aware of God and lingering in his presence.

---

3 Foster, Richard. 1992. *Prayer: Finding The True Hearts Home*. Harper: San Francisco

EIGHT

Prayer, it seemed, was simply a conversation
inside a relationship.

– Wm Paul Young

One of my favorite Bible stories is that of Elijah waiting for God on Mt. Horeb (1 Kings 19:11-13). Throughout the book of 1Kings God often speaks to Elijah in a clear, concise voice. In 1 Kings 18 and 19, God speaks to Elijah and tells him to go to Mt. Carmel then to Mt. Horeb.

Mt. Carmel was a magnificent event for Elijah. Here, on the top of the mountain he would have one of the largest audiences ever in his life. With poised confidence, he challenges the Baal prophets to a duel. With blatant arrogance, the Baal prophets accept the challenge: the first god to rain down fire upon the sacrificial altar would be the winner.

The Baal prophets go first and spend all morning and most of the afternoon calling upon their gods. Elijah was thoroughly enjoying this dinner show. At one point he begins to taunt them, "…shout louder…perhaps he is deep in thought or traveling…maybe your god is sleeping …" (1 Kings 18:27 paraphrased).

After hours of pleading to their gods, they finally give up. Elijah steps forward and calls upon God to act. God does so by performing a mighty miracle. He sends fire down from Heaven to consume a waterlogged sacrifice. Immediately the Israelites bow down and worship Jehovah. Elijah, in all of his glory, has over 400 Baal prophets killed. What a mountain top experience for Elijah!

We don't know the full emotional state of Elijah during this time, but his previous actions show him as a prophet obediently listening to God's voice and doing what God says, with positive results. Each time Elijah moved on to the next adventure he was confident that God would act, and he would reap the rewards of being an obedient Prophet.

The difference this time is that maybe, just maybe, the events did not end on a happy note as Elijah might have been expecting. Suddenly he finds himself on the run because Queen Jezebel puts a contract out on him, and her army is in hot pursuit to kill him for the murder of the Baal prophets, and for embarrassing her.

Elijah leaves his servant and runs deep into the desert. Jezebel wants him dead, and he finds himself a wanted man, running for his life. Exhausted, he collapses beneath a tree and cries out to God to let him die. He ran into the desert knowing there is no water or food there. He is tired and beaten down. His desire is to die.

Does this sound like the Elijah we just read about in previous chapters? Evidently, life isn't turning out the way Elijah thought it would. But God wasn't finished with him. He sends an angel who brings him food and water. Then God instructs him to go to Mt. Horeb which was a forty day journey from where he was in the desert.

What was going through his mind during this long trek?

Was he looking over his shoulder wondering if

Jezebel's men were after him?

Did he think that this was the last chance for God to prove himself?

What we do know is that God didn't give up on him. After traveling for almost a month and a half, he finally reaches Mt. Horeb. But God tells him to go even further, to the top of the mountain and wait there. Now, after traveling for forty days then climbing to the top of this mountain, a very physically demanding trek, and crawling into a cave, he waits. He is mentally, physically, and possibly spiritually exhausted, but he does as he is told, and waits.

We don't know how long he waits before a great wind shakes the mountain. We do know that God is not in the wind.

Again Elijah waits.

Then a terrible earthquake rocks the mountain like never before and probably knocks him to the ground.

God was not in the earthquake.

Elijah pulls himself up and once again waits for God.

Suddenly, a terrible fire sweeps across the mountain, probably leaving him reeking of smoke.

I would think by this time, after surviving a tornado, an

earthquake, and a forest fire, Elijah may doubt his sanity for being on top of this mountain.

Looking across the vast mountain range Elijah stands up and with all of the strength he has, he waits.

Without warning, God passes by in a whisper, a still, small voice. Finally, he hears God's voice. His waiting brings him to an indescribable experience with God.

He could have raced down the mountain after the tornado.

But he waited.

Fear could have seized him during the horrific forest fire.

But he stood firm.

He could have blamed God for almost dying in an earthquake.

But he didn't. He knew God well enough to trust him.

It is interesting that God gets his attention by whispering to him. God didn't yell from Heaven. He grabbed Elijah's attention by quietly speaking to him in a *still, small,* voice. These three simple words in Hebrew have profound significance:

- Still (*daman* – "daw-man") has the connotation of a whisper or a calm sea as found in Psalm 107:29, "He stilled the storm to a whisper; the waves of the sea were hushed"
- Small (*daq* – "dak") means fine or thin like a strand of hair.
- Voice (*Qwol* – "kole") is from an unusual root word that means to "call aloud."

God spoke to Elijah in a voice loud enough for him to hear (*Qwol*), but soft enough (*daman*) that it was calming to his soul, yet he was forced to strain (*dak*) to listen carefully to God's voice.

God speaks to Elijah in a way that releases his fears, anxieties, and any unbelief, yet with an unmistakable voice. He let Elijah know without a doubt that it is God who is calling out to him. God's voice is calming, yet with a cutting edge that pierced through him. Elijah heard something yet he needed to focus and disregard any other distractions in order to listen to God's unique voice.

How does this story apply to you? Are you going to church Sunday–to–Sunday (your mountaintop), but acting differently throughout the week? Has your life somehow changed in a way you were not expecting? Things didn't turn out as Elijah had expected. He was accustomed to walking away a hero, but instead, he became a fugitive. Sometimes you may expect life to treat you the same every day.

When problems arise, are you quick to run away and find the answer on your own (a Humanistic–Christian characteristic), or do you wait on God? Remember that Elijah spent a quiet forty day pilgrimage seeking God; hungry for more of him.

AWARE

There is a resurgence of the Buddhist philosophy of *mindfulness*. Mindfulness is nothing more than the Biblical concept of awareness, a way of life that God proposed to us thousands of years before the introduction of Buddhism.

The psalmist sings out "Be still and know (be aware) that I am God" (Psalms 46:10). Being aware, or mindful, of our reality is nothing new. I am inclined to believe the

Buddhists took the mindful concept from the early believers' experience of becoming aware of God.

It is very difficult, if not impossible, to be aware of God when you have become desensitized to him by fleeing his presence and running to satisfy lazy, fleshly desires by sitting in front of the TV, computer monitor, or by keeping so busy you deliberately become too preoccupied to listen.

God has been mindful of reminding us for centuries that we can know him through being aware of his presence. He wants you to be in a continual awareness of his presence at all times:

- When you struggle, you know God is with you.
- When you are blessed, you know it is God who has prospered you.
- When you commune with him, you know it is God who responds and speaks to you.
- When you focus on God, you become aware of Him.

To be aware of God means to *consider* him. So what does it mean to consider something? You may consider a job proposal and think about the pros and cons of accepting the job. You may consider buying a car and you research the vehicle and think about your options. What you spend most of your time thinking about is what you value in life. Consider what the Bible says about what you value:

- "But be sure to fear the Lord and serve him faithfully with all your heart; *consider* what great things he has done for you." (1 Samuel 12:24)
- "Listen to this, Job; stop and *consider* God's wonders." (Job 37:14)
- "When I *consider* your heavens, the work of your fingers, the moon, and the stars, which you have set in place, what is man that you are mindful of him, the son of man that you care for or him?" (Psalms 8:3-9)
- "I will meditate on all your works and *consider* all your mighty deeds."(Psalms 77:12)
- "Whoever is wise, let him heed these things and

consider the great love of the Lord."

(Psalms 107: 43)

These few verses direct us to be perpetually mindful of God's presence. The problem that plagues most Christians is the distractions of noise, sights, tastes, and other fleshly desires. Our thoughts (our considerations) must be focused on him.

Where are your thoughts focused?

NINE

Prayer is not monologue, but dialogue.
– Andrew Murray

The early believers understood the human as a holistic being. Worship was not separated from any other aspect of life. Their physical world functioned in sync with the spiritual world. It is problematic for some believers today to fully grasp the depth of their physio-spiritual makeup. Psalm 63:1 expresses it this way: "O God, you are my God, earnestly I seek you; my soul thirsts for you, my body longs for you." I think it is very interesting that the psalmist uses the word *body* (in other versions, the word *flesh* is used). It isn't just our mind that longs for him; it should be our entire being.

The Hebrew understanding of worship was a lifestyle, a continual act, rather than a separate event. The Old Testament Hebrew would not understand the programmed worship found in most postmodern churches.

DOING GOD'S WORK

We sometimes run as far as we can to avoid waiting. Sometimes where we run is straight to church. Quite often much of our time is spent *doing*. Some of you are being *Church–atized* – spending much of your time attending a multitude of church functions, thinking that you must be *doing* for God instead of getting to *know* God.

Critics may ask, "Is this a bad thing?" No, it isn't. But the problem arises when there is no balance between your contemplative time with God and your fellowship time with other believers and commitment to church matters. You do need the interaction and knowledge from your spiritual leaders and friends. But, you also need our quiet times with God. The act of quiet is an integral part of discipline in your spiritual life.

I lost count, in my thirty plus years in the ministry of how many times I heard people tell me that they love doing God's work, but hate being alone. How is it possible to listen to God if you never stop? Many Christians feel good that they can do something at their church. It is most definitely God's will for us to do good things for him, but you must balance our life with times of quiet to listen.

When do you have time to listen to God? With raw candor Thomas Merton addresses this issue:

"There are men dedicated to God whose lives are full of restlessness and who have no real desire to be alone. They admit that exterior solitude is good in theory. In practice, their lives are devoured by activities and strangled with attachments. Interior solitude is impossible for them. They fear it. They are great promoters of useless work. They love to organize meetings and banquets and conferences and lectures. They print circulars, write letters, talk for hours on the telephone in order that they may gather a hundred people together in a large room where they roar at one another and clap their hands and stagger home at last patting one another on the back with assurance they have all done great things to spread the Kingdom of

God."[1]

There can be no contemplation, no contentment, no commitment, and no consideration of God's grace and love for you when you are so busy doing that you can't hear him. Entering into the spiritual realm is challenging if not impossible without pause. How then can you come into God's presence when you have a restless spirit that causes you to be devoured by activities and strangled with attachments?

GOD STEALING TIME

You steal time from God by rejecting his invitation.

I often hear people say, "I wish I had more time to pray." Conversation is not a duty or item on your checklist to complete, it should invade your life. Again, do you forget or overlook the substance of Scripture? In 1 Thessalonians 5:16-18 Paul says that you are to pray continually: "Rejoice always, *pray continually,* give thanks in all circumstances; for this is God's will for you in Christ Jesus." Not just during your devotional but throughout the day.

---

1 Merton

This is relational conversation.

Time is either an obstacle you abuse by missing out on God's amazing blessings, or it is the wonderful gift you accept to sit in quiet with him. Every day you are offered a choice to use your time wisely. What you choose is a reflection of our spiritual temperament.

Do you steal valuable time from God?

Do you choose to be with God or do you choose to be without God?

So, how do you live a disciplined life? The first question to ask is: "Do I want to follow God or not?" Once you have determined that you are willing to take up your cross, then you are able to honestly start your journey to a deeper intimacy with God.

In our adrenaline rush culture we are calendar–dependent. Our lives revolve around appointments, schedules, and deadlines. Industries have been created to help people manage their calendar–dependency.

We live by agendas, whether it is work, school, or family, and we are confined to timelines. This in itself is not problematic; it's simply the way life is for most people.

However, if conversing with God is not in your calendar–driven lifestyle, are you any better than other religions that *hope* they make it to Heaven? You *hope* that God will answer your prayer, instead of listening and knowing what he has to say.

The paradox is that there is a hesitation to become absorbed by God in fear of losing out on momentary affections of pleasure. It is easier to miss time with him than your TV agenda.

When you steal time from God, you become desensitized to the passion he has for you. God–conversation is the act of crossing from the physical to the spiritual world. There should come a time when both are synchronized.

Leonard Ravenhill was one of the greatest evangelists to come out of England in the 1900's. Near the end of his life he makes this stirring remark: "If I had spent more time alone with God rather than preaching and planning how I was going to change the world, I would be a very different man."[2] Keep in mind that this is a man who spent at least two hours a day

2 Tomlinson, Mack. 2010. *In Light of Eternity*, The Life of Leonard Ravenhill. Free Grace Press: Conway, AR

in conversation with God.

Consider the analogy of a cup filled to one–half with water. This represents the busy Christian whose lifestyle is comprised of work, relaxation, reading their Bible, going to church, and praying. Sound familiar? However, the more you develop your relationship with God the more the water rises in the cup and the more you are filled with him, and the act of conversation becomes ongoing, continual, and unceasing. The less time you spend developing your relationship with God, the less water is in the cup.

Don't you want your cup to overflow?

DUO TASKING

In our crazy, busy, ADD culture people brag about multitasking. Even the origination of the name, *multiple tasking,* is compounded to make it easier to pronounce. Doing multiple tasks at one time can seriously affect your ultimate goal because each time you introduce a new object into what you are doing, you dilute your attention to any one of the objects. If your goal is to have an intimate relationship with God, how do you accomplish this when you dilute your attention with the soft glow of your computer screen while changing the channel on your TV, while talking to your friends on your cell phone?

Our culture has created a multitasking environment. Sometimes you need to multi-task, and sometimes you need to stop. Multitasking can be addicting. Longing for God often takes a back seat to a busy lifestyle, and you become God–deficit. You can become passionless towards God.

As a Christian, you should be *duo–tasking*: doing two things at the same time. We live in a physical world, but we have access to the spiritual world. Duo–tasking is the obligation of every believer to live in the physical world and to be aware of God continually. Many of us try to duo–task only when we are in a fellowship gathering. Throughout the week we forget that God is always waiting for us to hear him. He longs to give us direction, to shower us with his love, to allow us to be used by him.

People are hurting and needful all around us, sometimes within arm's reach. How can you be listening for God's purpose if you are only living in the physical world? Whether at work, recreation, or alone, you should be tuned into God always duo-tasking.

Jesus is the model you should use to live a lifestyle of worship. Everything about Jesus was duo–tasking. He lived in the physical world but was continually listening to his Father (an act of unceasing conversation). Here is a closer look at Jesus duo–tasking in *Conversation,* in *Conflict*, and in *Crisis*:

Conversation

The story of the Samaritan woman he meets at a well (John 4) is a prime example of duo–tasking. He meets her (physical world) and while they are talking Jesus is listening to his Father (spiritual world). God reveals to Jesus that this woman was married five times and the man she is living with is not her husband.

How would he know this?

Conflict

The story of the woman caught in adultery is a well–known story found in John 8:1-11. Jesus is confronted by some Scribes and Pharisees trying to trick him. These religious men were confident that this would be the opportune time to finally trip him up, prove that they were the ultimate authority. While they tried to press him on the law, he simply listened to his father and did as he was told: *write in the dirt.* The words written on the dry, dusty ground startled them and one by one they slipped away.

How did he know what to write?

Crisis

Did you ever consider why Jesus said nothing to Herod prior to his crucifixion (Luke 23:9)? Before you answer that question, consider what he said in John 6:38, "For I have come down from heaven not to do my will but to do the will of him who sent me." How would he know to be silent unless he heard from his Father and honored his will? Can you picture this scene? Luke 23 gives us a picture of the Chief Priests and scribe "accusing him *vehemently*" yet he said nothing.

In a crisis of life or death, what prompted him to stay silent?

When you have a *conversation* are you duo–tasking?

When you have a *conflict,* an argument for example,

do you duo–task?

When you are in a *crisis* what is your first response?

Can you duo–task?

If Jesus can duo–task, why can't you?

Be available.

Be aware.

Listen.

TEN

*In prayer, you encounter God not only in the small voice
and the soft breeze, but also in the midst of
the turmoil of the world.*

– Henri Nouwen

It was my turn to pick the kids up at school. My seven–
year–old daughter, Nikki, piled into the backseat and wrestled
with her backpack until she was able to thrust it to the floor.

"I'm not going back to school," she announced.

Surprised by this declaration, I shifted my body
and turned to look at her straight on. I was concerned that
something might have happened to her.

"Oh, why aren't you going back to school?" I asked.

"I know everything there is to know, so I don't need
school."

"Really?" I said, now intrigued and armed with fatherly wisdom to teach her a simple lesson. "Well," I continued, "If you know so much, what is eight times seven?"

"Dad! We haven't learned that yet."

"Ok. How about something else?" She began to fidget but was ready for the fight. My wife grew up in Washington State, so I thought I would give her an easy question: "What is the capital of Washington?"

Her eyes narrowed, and she folded her arms in defiance. She pondered the question for a moment then blurted out, "W!"

Well, I couldn't fault her for that answer. Maybe she did know it all... at least in that moment in time. In her mind she was right. Nikki is a straight A student and might have felt bored that day. Nikki is now much older and understands more about life and that the capital of Washington is Olympia.

I've often thought back to that day and pondered, *'Have I learned everything there is to know in God's school? Do I understand his relationship with me?'*

How do you view God? Do you hear and converse openly with him? Sometimes our understanding of God can be like understanding what the capital of Washington is. We understand God is our creator but is that all there is?

The act of hearing God involves a significant act of physical and mental discipline. Throughout the New Testament, Paul speaks of self–control and discipline. It is interesting that the Paul uses athletic training for many of his parallels:

- "No discipline seems pleasant at the time, but painful. Later on, however, it produces a harvest of righteousness and peace for those who have been trained by it" (Hebrew 12:11).
- "Therefore, since we are surrounded by such a great cloud of witnesses, let us throw off everything that hinders and the sin that so easily entangles. And let us run with perseverance the race marked out for us, fixing our eyes on Jesus, the pioneer, and perfecter of faith" (Hebrews 12:1,2).
- "Do you not know that those who run in a race all

run, but only one receives the prize? Run in such a way that you may win. Everyone who competes in the games exercises self–control in all things. They then do it to receive a perishable wreath, but we an imperishable. Everyone who competes in the games goes into strict training. They do it to get a crown that will not last, but we do it to get a crown that will last forever" (1 Corinthians 9:24- 25 – NASB).

- "Therefore I run in such a way, as not without aim; I box in such a way, as not beating the air; but I discipline my body and make it my slave, so that, after I have preached to others, I myself will not be disqualified." (1 Corinthians 9:26–27 - NASB).

- "Similarly, anyone who competes as an athlete does not receive the victor's crown except by competing according to the rules" (2 Timothy 2:5).

- "I have fought the good fight, I have finished the race, I have kept the faith" (2 Timothy 4:7).

The comparison Paul is referring to is that of an Olympic athlete. The athletes of this period weren't much different than those of our contemporary Olympic hopefuls; fame and fortune follow the victor. The Roman and Greek athlete trained rigorously to obtain a victory so coveted it could mean early retirement, wealth, and fame for the rest of his life.

In some cities, the winner of the Olympic games was treated with such prestige that a hole would be made in the outer wall and the victor would be led in on a chariot by four white horses. Depending on who the ruler was, some champions had statues erected and strategically placed in the busiest part of the city.

The only name ever recorded at an Olympic event was the winner. There was no second or third place; no bronze or silver. Therefore, the goal of the athlete was to commit to a regimented, disciplined life of training to win. Each day was filled with an organized schedule of events. His meals were planned, his exercise demanding, and most importantly, he abstained from anything that might corrupt his training. He pushed his body to the limits of endurance. He kept his goal focused on the prize. A person with a strong commitment to thorough and extensive training could obtain riches by adhering to a regimented lifestyle. The correlation he draws is that of a spiritual versus a physical training:

They do it to get a crown. Originally, the victor's crown was made from olive leaves from sacred olive trees near the temple of Zeus. The crown eventually wilted and died unlike a crown of gold that will last forever.

And let us run with perseverance the race marked out for us, fixing our eyes on Jesus. The runner's eyes were focused on the course track for any ruts, stones or any other objects that might hinder his performance. He must also know where the boundaries and his opponents were at all times. If he were to look into the crowd, he may lose his balance or run off the track. It was imperative that the runner kept his concentration and eyes on the course. Likewise, you are to focus on God and listen to him.

I do not fight like a man beating the air. A boxer who was not in shape or thoroughly trained in the art of boxing could easily throw punches that connected with nothing but air. Paul's visual is a boxer swinging his arms and flailing at the air. In contrast, the trained boxer is in top physical condition and prepared to go the distance with his opponent.

"No, I beat my body and make it my slave."

When you abstain from TV for time with God, spend more time in conversation rather than Tweeting, or when you fast or give financially to those in need when you are struggling yourself then you are disciplining your spiritual bodies. A lot can be gleaned about discipline with the athlete analogy. You are to focus on the goal of eternal life with God.

With that in mind, a spiritual life needs to be a disciplined life. More importantly, Paul's emphasis is that you are to covet God and live a disciplined lifestyle of conversation.

However, discipline often means change.

Henri Nouwen says, "...prayer requires discipline. Discipline means to create boundaries around our meeting with God."[1] A concentrated effort is imperative because holy conversation is not familiar to our natural responses or habits. You must make it so familiar that you can't function without it.

One reason some people don't make the right changes

1 Nouwen, Henri. 1999. *The Only Necessary Thing: living a prayerful life.* The Crossroads Publishing Company: NY

in their life is the cost of doing something like listening to God, which means concentrating on something other than the television or computer.

Discipline equals the expenditure of energy.

INTRUDING ON SILENCE

The early believers understood the importance of meditation. To them, meditate meant: enter into the quiet, the silent. Many Believers today live their lives continually intruding on silence as if it were a path to be trampled instead of an experience to be embraced.

When you entertain thoughts of rationalization (ie. *I'm tired, God wants me to relax, I'll get a round–tuit later*) you have already become complacent. This is an indicator of your lack of passion, and your loss of perseverance. You can't run the race or fight the fight and when trials come you throw up your hands and cry to God, "Where are you?"

Intruding on silence is escaping intimacy with God.

Remember: Be still and know.

It is not enough just to be still. Buddhist monks can discipline their minds to be still. But God wants you take stillness a step further by being silent so that you can *experience* him.

Why is it difficult to be quiet?

What is preventing you from stopping? Hurry–and–Scurry is in direct opposition to God's desire for us to Stop–and–Listen.

I think of the harried mother who rises, sometimes in the middle of the night, to care for a crying baby. Exhaustion pounds at her head. Sleep escapes her. Responsibility and nurture meet her with every coo and cry. Finding time to stop is not easy, and you are not to forsake your obligations. But you must find that time to spend with your Father.

There is no escaping the reality that you live in a noise–filled world. How you cope with noise and distractions is the choice you must make. When coming home from an exhausting day, it may help to let your spouse and children know that you need ten minutes or half an hour to be alone.

Susanna Wesley, the mother of evangelists Charles and John Wesley, had a unique way of finding time alone with God in the busyness of life. Living in a home with over ten children she would sit down at the dinner table and pull her apron up over her head. She would use this time to pray. Her children knew this was her alone time and not to disturb her. Susanna understood the need for quiet and time with God. She sought it and focused her attention on God.

IN THE COMPANY OF TREES AND WATERFALLS

Sometimes your lifestyle may not always give you the opportunity to find a quiet place. Distractions can tempt us away from distinctly hearing God's voice. It would be wonderful if we could have a library experience where quiet was everywhere. However, that is rarely the case even though we need to experience quiet, you also need to hear God in the noise of your life.

My friend, Jesse, helped a mutual friend learn to listen to God's voice through a unique but effective lesson. Jesse took a friend, who I will call Gabe, to the woods, and the two spent quality time in the company of trees and of God. In the solitude of the woods, Gabe was elated that he could finally hear God's voice. But Jesse wasn't quite finished with Gabe. Jesse then took him to one of Central Oregon's beautiful waterfalls. Standing as close as they could to the falls Jesse instructed Gabe to be quiet and listen for God's voice. After a quick five minutes, Gabe cried, "I can't hear anything but the rushing falls!"

A large rock jutted from the pool at the bottom of the falls and Jesse said, "Focus on the water hitting the rock at the bottom of the falls."

Gabe closed his eyes and focused on the sound and after a couple of minutes acknowledged that he could hear the water crashing against the rock.

"Now, listen to the bird singing."

"What bird? I don't hear any bird," Gabe exclaimed.

"Listen."

Frustrated, but determined to hear God's voice, Gabe again closed his eyes. Soon his lips curled upwards, and he softly said, "I hear it."

Jesse quietly responded, "You have heard the sound of the water hitting the rock and you heard one single bird singing all as you stand at the bottom of these falls. You focused your attention away from what you didn't want to hear to what was important for you to hear."

If you truly want to know God intimately, how will

you discipline your life?

Energy equates to physical and emotional discipline. It takes energy to rise from you chair and fall on your knees. Could it be this is why Charles Templeton, Katy Perry, George Perdikis, and others deconverted? Maybe they weren't willing to expend the energy to seek after him.

It's not difficult.

It's a choice.

It's an amazing, wonderful expenditure of energy to be in God's presence.

God's passion is that you are passionate for him; that you run, not walk (become complacent) to him. Ponder this from Hebrews 12:1, "Therefore, since we are surrounded by so great a cloud of witnesses, let us also lay aside every weight, and sin which clings so closely, and let us run with endurance the race that is set before us" (English Standard Version.). The Greek word for endurance can also be translated as *patient*. Run with patience. It sounds contradictive, doesn't it? The word *run* also has the meaning of *to spend one's strength in performing or attaining something.*

It's wonderful to hear God when we are alone and quiet; we need these times. However, duo–tasking is more about *continual* conversation with God than location. Jesus was always in touch with God.

What is keeping you from doing what Jesus did?

ELEVEN

The trouble with nearly everybody who prays is that he says
'Amen' and runs away before God has a chance
to reply. Listening to God is far more
important than giving Him our ideas.

– Frank Laubach

How and why you converse with God isn't as important as *desire*. It is not until you have set in motion the decision to modify your thoughts, senses, and emotions that you can experience God. What type of relationship would you have with your spouse or friends that consisted of nothing more than you talking and never listening? Undoubtedly the relationship wouldn't last. This is not conversation it is prideful negotiation.

I don't confess to being a huge Shakespeare fan but I

have read some of his works, and one of my favorite quotes comes from *Hamlet* where King Claudius cries out, "*My words fly up, my thoughts remain below: Words without thoughts never to heaven go.*"

How is it possible to entertain the thought of spending eternity with God when your one–sided conversations have no depth or connection, no focus or faith. You continually toss prayers to God but there is no substance. Some Christians like to cut and paste prayers into the situation they want others to hear:

"…give them traveling mercies…"

"…we pray a hedge of protection…"

"…bless this food we are about to partake…"

There is nothing fundamentally wrong with these cut and paste prayers, but it is not just about the words you speak, it's about the relationship you have with the one you are carrying on the conversation with.

Do you converse with God or only petition him?

Some approach conversation with God as if they were phoning in a pizza order. They quickly make their requests known and hang up. To these people, waiting can seem like a mind–numbing experience. But those that choose to wait and listen experience an awakening of their soul.

Conversation with God can take different forms but all lead to intimacy with him. Conversation begins with you quieting yourself before God. It is in stillness that we create a space for God to invade us, hear us, and converse with us.

The most common methods of conversation are *Lifestyle Conversation, Intercessory Conversation, Contemplative Conversation, and Centering Conversation* (however, Centering Conversation is more focused on the act of conversation). Although there is no form or right or wrong way of conversing with God it is easier to understand the mortal functions you engage in to develop a more affectionate and familiar relationship with him.

LIFESTYLE CONVERSATION

Frank Laubach was an American missionary to the Philippines. Laubach's legacy was to inspire believers to constantly be aware of God. Laubach believed whole-heartedly in conversing with God continually basing his theology on 1 Thessalonians 5:17, "Rejoice always, pray continually, give thanks in all circumstances; for this is God's will for you in Christ Jesus." He stressed that we should converse or at least be aware of God every minute of every day.

The words *always* and *continually* from this scripture are active, ongoing directives. Laubach published a pamphlet he called *The Game With Minutes*[1], in which he lays out a program to keep ever mindful of God by keeping track of how often you think of God. He goes into practical detail on how to achieve a more intimate relationship with God by changing habits to consider God at all times. He suggests using a small notepad that you can slip into your pocket or purse. Each time you think of God make a tick on your notepad. At the end of the day count up the number of ticks. This is an excellent exercise to get you into the habit of being aware of God.

When you interact with the world whether it is at work, a luncheon, school, the grocery store, or wherever you are during the day, you can enter into a *Lifestyle Conversation* with God. Your goal should be to duo–task: listen to God

---

1 Laubauch, Frank. 2012. *The Game With Minutes*. Martino Fine Books: Eastford, CT

as you interact with those you come in contact with. The opportunity to duo–task is an exercise in building our spiritual muscles. At first you may have difficulty, but God is there to pick you up and offer grace. Soon you will be able to hear his voice even as you are conversing with others.

INTERCESSORY CONVERSATION

Intercession is as much about compassion as it is about conversation. Intercession is the act of bringing the needs of others into God's presence. Henri Nouwen explains intercession like this: "To pray, therefore, is to become those for whom we pray, to become the sick child, the fearful mother, the distressed father, the nervous teenager, the angry student… To pray is to enter into a deep solidarity with our fellow human beings so that in and through us they can be touched by the healing power of God's Spirit."[2]

So how does intercession help me know God or hear his voice? As you consider the spiritual health of someone for salvation, healing, or financial provision you step outside of our selfish desires and seek God with a purpose. Picture yourself

---

2 Nouwen

standing before God with the person you are interceding for. Consider the feelings, the hurt, and the despair of the person you have brought with you before God.

Compassion will begin to rise within you and God will become your focus. However, if you toss up a prayer without true compassion you are no better than a rock trying to fling itself into the air.

You can toss up words of concern to God on behalf of someone without much thought or understanding. Intercessory conversation is not to be taken lightly. Sometimes the need of the person you are interceding for becomes an emotional plea to God instead of a conversation. True intercession is first entering into God's presence and then bringing your need (intercession) to him. You are not just meeting God, you are experiencing being in his presence..

In Daniel chapter nine we find an example of intercessory conversation. Daniel acknowledges to God that he is aware of God's character and humbly comes before him. It is here that Daniel opens his heart to intimacy. He intercedes to ask God to forgive a nation that has sinned. He asks God to withhold his wrath against an entire nation. But as you read through this passage in Daniel notice what he says to God in this conversation:

- "Lord, the great and awesome God, who keeps his covenant of love with those who love him and keep his commandments" (9:4).
- "...Lord, you are righteous" (9:7).
- "The Lord our God is merciful and forgiving" (9:9).
- "...the Lord our God is righteous in everything he does" (9:1.)
- "...we do not make requests of you because we are righteous, but because of your great mercy" (9:18).

Daniel's words flew up but so did his thoughts – straight from his heart. He recognized that God is awesome, merciful, forgiving, and righteous. This is not a reminder to God, but an acknowledgment of the past, present, and future greatness of God. Daniel's spirit touched God.

True intimate communion took place.

CONTEMPLATIVE CONVERSATION

Contemplative conversation is simply spending time considering and seeking God. It is often associated with meditation and sometimes used interchangeably. To put into perspective a concise definition of contemplation, Teresa of Avila said it like this, "Contemplative prayer in my opinion is nothing else than a close sharing between friends; it means taking time frequently to be alone with him who we know loves us." Trappist monk, Thomas Merton adds his thoughts, "Contemplation goes beyond concepts and apprehends God not as a separate object but as the Reality within our reality."

The act of being still, being quiet, and focusing on God alone is contemplation.

Contemplation allows you to consider God and how wonderful he is. It also forces you to stop and offer to him your time and obedience.

CENTERING CONVERSATION

When you are not interceding or seeking conversational personal petitions you are offering contemplative conversation. Trappist monks Thomas Keating and Basil Pennington have separately resuscitated the ancient tradition of Centering Prayer. Although the name may imply a different concept of conversation, it is an insight into the physical and spiritual aspects of conversing with God. Centering Conversation is not a Buddhist mantra or a series of rote prayers. Rather the intent is to be actively present in God's presence.

In his insightful book, *Open Mind, Open Heart*[3] Keating offers practical advice on how to more effectively converse with our God. He suggests establishing guidelines for effective conversation:

- First choose a sacred word as the symbol of your intention to consent to God's presence and action within. The sacred word expresses our intention to consent to God's presence and action within. It is chosen during a brief period of prayer to the Holy Spirit. Use a word of one or two syllables, such as God, Jesus, Abba, Amen, Love, Listen, Peace,

---

3 Keating, Thomas. 2006. *Open Mind, Open Heart.* Bloomsbury Academic: London

Mercy, Let Go, Silence, Stillness, Faith, or Trust.

- Next, sitting comfortably and with eyes closed, settle briefly and silently introduce the sacred word as the symbol of your consent to God's presence and action within. When engaged with your thoughts, return ever so gently to the sacred word. During Centering Conversation, the sacred word may become vague or disappear.

- At the end of the prayer period, remain in silence with eyes closed for a couple of minutes. The additional two minutes enables us to bring the atmosphere of silence into everyday life.

In addition to Keating's practical advice, it is important to note two other items related to Centering Conversation: *Internal* and *External*.

Internal: when you close your eyes you may see a theater of life events scroll across the screen. Your thoughts will tug at you to flee the moment to experience something other than God's presence. They may come in the form of future plans, previous events, current issues, or simply daydreams. It is at this moment you must use the sacred word to draw your attention back to God.

External: for most of us it is impossible to live in a world void of noise. Therefore it's important to understand that God can speak to you in the busiest, loudest environments of our day. You can learn to accept the noise instead of fighting it by recognizing it. As mentioned earlier, while you are conversing you may hear a dog bark, or a car go by, the ticking of a clock, the wind, or a multitude of other noises. When this occurs simply say, "I recognize the wind is blowing," or "I recognize a dog is barking."

Healthcare is continually researching the holistic treatment of patients. Biofeedback and meditation have historically been at the forefront of non-traditional healing practices. However, a 2009 pilot study of women receiving chemotherapy for recurrent ovarian cancer using Centering Prayer (Conversation) concluded that most participants identified centering prayer as beneficial. Emotional well–being, anxiety, depression, and faith scores showed improvement.[4] Although this was only a pilot study, it's

---

4 Retrieved from: *https://asu.pure.elsevier.com*

interesting to note that prayer is being considered as an alternative healing aid. Of course, Christianity has known this for millennia.

Being aware of your surroundings and our thoughts enables you to turn your focus back to God. The more you practice seeking God, the more intimacy is developed. You can't all spend your days in the quiet woods or a silent monastery. But you can spend time in God's presence anywhere, anytime.

AMEN!

Just for a moment consider this short, rote intercessory cry: "God, please heal Jane of her cancer. Amen." Or, "God, Bill is in desperate need of paying his bills. Please help him. Amen." Now look at these two requests backwards.

First, most of us end our conversations with *amen*. It was a custom, which was passed over from the synagogues to the Christian assemblies, that when someone had offered up solemn prayer to God, the others responded *amen*, and thus made the substance of what was uttered their own. They took ownership and agreed that God would act.

In chapter eight of the book of Nehemiah, we discover that the Israelites have just finished rebuilding the walls of Jerusalem. We find the people gathered together, standing in the square, praising God and that they were of one accord, or "one man' (just as the believers were in Acts 2).

Ezra brought out the Book of the Law and began to read from it. When he finished he blessed God, and in unison, all of the people shouted, "Amen!" which means: so be it! we are in agreement!" Or as the Millenials would say, "Right?"

After declaring their ownership in their amen, they fell to the ground and worshiped God (*proskunetes*). With reckless abandonment to their outward appearance, they fell in the dust, the dirt, and the mud.

They weren't looking around to see who was watching.

They simply worshiped God.

They made the blessing of God their own.

They connected with God.

They took ownership in the proclamation Ezra offered to God.

When I was a child we said amen in our church so much that it became an impersonal rote ritual. At the close of the service our pastor would often say, "And all the people said (from Nehemiah 8)…" and the congregation responded with a loud, "Amen!"

The close of the service was around noon and by that time of day I was becoming very hungry. So, in my childish imagination I always wished the ritual would have gone something like this:

Pastor: "And all the people said…."

Congregation: "Let's order pizza!"

The Hebrew word for *amen* is associated with the word *aman* which is the English word *believe*. Amen is a personal, intimate covenant which you make with God that ushers you into his presence. Here you stand before him and declare that you believe with all of your heart that your request has been made known. The word *amen* is not a period at the end of a conversation with God, it is an exclamation point. It is a declaration to God, "I believe you will act!" It is taking ownership in the conversation with God.

Have you ever heard people say, "We need to pray harder?" God doesn't want you to speak to him with intensity. He wants you to speak to him with intimacy. Jesus and Paul use the word *abba* to describe an intimacy with God (see Mark 13:46, Romans 8:15, Galatians 4:6). They both interceded with experience because they knew God intimately.

What is keeping you from knowing God intimately?

HOW TO

TWELVE

*We shall never know the mind of God till we learn
to know the voice of God.*

– Smith Wigglesworth

You have made it this far. So, are you ready to put into
practice the act of knowing God?

Let's start by answering a simple question: what are
characteristics of a healthy relationship between a spouse or
friend? Most people would answer with quick snippets like
open and honest communication, trust, respect, and *love.* And
they would be correct.

But have you considered your communication with God?
Is the communication one–way? Do you stop to listen to what
was spoken to you? Do you only hope? Hope that the relationship
continues while you petition him but don't take the time to listen.

These are certainly not characteristics that would deepen a relationship. Quite the opposite it would weaken and stunt the dynamics between the two parties. Sadly, many Christians have this type of relationship with God. They want God to act but only hope that he will because they are unwilling to hear what he has to say. Many Religions base their belief in hope. Muslims *hope* they will get to Heaven. Buddhists *hope* they can achieve enlightenment.

So, what is the difference between what you believe and what they believe? Is it based on hoping that if you live a good life and go to church that you will get to heaven? Is entrance into Heaven your only goal? You may have heard Christians say, "I know that I know that I know!" Why don't they say, "I experience God that I experience God that I experience God?"

We know what we know, but do we experience what we experience with God in a healthy relationship? The difference between the Humanistic–Christian and the Passionate Believer is *experience*.

Knowing God is *experiencing* him on a daily basis.

What if you never took time to develop a relationship

with your spouse or friend? All you did was talk about yourself? The same concept is often played out with Christians every day. No honest and open communication and no trust; just a hope that you will get a Willy Wonka Golden Ticket to Heaven.

Hearing God's voice is an experience you will never forget. But to clearly hear him you must first *desire* to hear him and know that it may come with a change in your lifestyle.

We have become a people who intercede and petition God but are afraid to listen to him for fear of missing out on a fleeting moment of earthly attention. Attention is what draws us to or away from God.

Military personnel *stand* at attention to give their full respect to the person in front of them.

The plot of a movie or television program *grabs* your attention.

The Internet *tugs* at your intellect and emotions pulling your attention towards it. What you focus or concentrate on is what you will best expend your energy on.

Emily Maroutian explains energy like this, "Energy

is the currency of the universe. When you 'pay' attention to something you buy that experience…Be selective in your focus because your attention feeds the energy and keeps it alive…"[1]

You will find in Revelation 3:20 a promise that if you stop, quiet your heart, and listen he will speak, "Here I am! I stand at the door and knock. If anyone *hears* my voice and opens the door, I will come in and eat with him, and he with me." This promise is more than just listening; he wants to spend time with you. It is an analogy of two people relaxing, conversing, and enjoying their time together.

Do you make time to unwind, settle back, and converse with God? How you spend your time is a direct reflection on your relationship with God.

ARE YOU LISTENING?

You must learn how to give God your attention.
When a parent asks a child, "Are you listening?" it is usually because the demeanor of the child seems inattentive. If the

---

1 Maroutian, Emily. *The Energy of Emotions: The 10 Emotional Environments and How They Shape The World Around Us*. CreateSpace Independent Publishing Platform (March 21, 2015)

child were attentive, he or she would be focused on what the parent is saying. If you approach focused conversation with God, in the same manner, you will enter into a healthy relationship.

Writers on the discipline of meditation, such as Richard Foster and James Finley share that while preparing to meditate one should be aware of distractions. The key to blocking out these noises is to recognize that there are *distractions*. Once you have recognized there is something keeping you from God's presence acknowledge it and bring your thoughts back to God (Philippians 4:8). There is no right or wrong way to converse with God. Position, place, or methodologies are not as important as the condition of your heart.

LIFE EXPERIENCES

Life experience can keep you from clearly hearing God. He is, and always been, available to talk to you but your experiences can create obstacles that stand in your way in developing a healthy relationship with him.

Here are some Life Experiences you may face:

Woundings. I have worked with many Christians who have been hurt by pastors, elders, and other Christians. These unresolved hurts are a filter to hearing God clearly.

What you see in the natural. Logic is often our reasoning for not hearing, or better yet, wanting to hear him. God may be speaking to you on a specific issue but you can't see how you could do it (logically) so you don't.

Your emotions. Feelings can often be strong filters that you use to approach God. They can also disguise themselves as truth. When you want to make a large purchase (i.e. TV, car, house, etc.), you may *feel* that a particular item is what God is telling you to buy when in reality it is your own feelings that are getting in the way. Now you may be thinking, 'How do I know? It seems too hard to distinguish between my thoughts/feelings and God's voice.' This is where discipline comes into action.

Keep reading.

Where your heart is. If you are not living the way you know you should, how will you hear from God? Sin is the biggest culprit of filtering God's voice. Consider Amos 3:3 "Do two walk together unless they have agreed to do so?"

and Isaiah 59:2 "But your iniquities have separated you from your God; your sins have hidden his face from you so that he will not hear." And as mentioned earlier, complacency is the enemy's tool that hinders an intimate relationship with God.

Sometimes it's difficult to recognize how you hear God's voice. So, he speaks to us through many different venues. He can speak to you through the Bible, dreams and visions, experiences and encounters. But there is nothing like hearing his voice.

STOP IN THE NAME OF his LOVE

It is vital to understand that to have an intimate, life-changing experience with God you may have to make lifestyle changes. Sometimes habits are not easy to change.

This is why people run away from God.

So, don't become dependent on others in hearing God's voice for you. It's one thing to get confirmation about something you are conversing with God about, and another to hear his voice on your own.

If you are not deepening your relationship with God and spending time with him then there is a problem that you need to immediately address. Do not let a day go by without talking with him.

Keep trying.

If you have doubt, then you need to spend more time pursuing him. If you keep seeking out others for the answer you will never grow past where you are. You will never experience him for yourself.

What are some *Holy Habits* you can put into practice?

THIRTEEN

I am doing what I shall do through all eternity – blessing God, praising God, adoring God, giving Him the love of my whole heart. It is our one business, my brethren, to worship Him and love him without thought of anything else.

– Brother Lawrence

My friend's daughter, Julie, was teaching her first grade Sunday school class on bringing all your concerns to God in prayer. She told the class that they could pray if they were sad, or sick, or lost. To which one little boy quickly replied, "Miss Julie, I don't have to pray if I'm lost. I just use my cell phone."

How often do you try to take the easy route to God? God does not have call waiting. But he has waiting for us to seek him. His pleasure is watching us pursue him, long for him, and desire to be with him.

GET (ME) OUT OF MY WAY!

So, how can you change your lifestyle? Get away to a place where you can be intentional to listen to Gods voice. Get rid of your distractions. Begin to make lifestyle changes that will include more time with God.

God wants your time.

Don't steal it from him.

Changing your lifestyle is not easy. But if you truly desire to know God more intimately, you must own the distractions that are keeping you from him.

The more time I spend with him, the less I desire my (old) distractions. Find your place to get quiet with God. It is up to you to hear God's voice for yourself. He wants to speak to you and is waiting to for you to seek a more fulfilling relationship with him. But give yourself grace. It will take time to hear his voice; how much time depends on you.

Just keep going.

Don't give up even if you don't hear anything at first. You will if you continue to put this into practice. In the early stages of your journey, it may best to seek out someone you know who hears God clearer than you.

VERB

Paul challenged the church in Corinth to continually examine their motives, *Examine yourselves to see whether you are in the faith; test yourselves. Do you not realize that Christ Jesus is in you--unless, of course, you fail the test?* (2 Corinthians 13:5). Remember that faith comes from hearing and God longs for us to pursue him.

Get out of the way.

Allow God to be God.

Ask him what areas in your life need improving. Is there any sin you aren't aware of? See what areas could use improvement.

MAKE TIME!

Set aside hours, or at first, minutes. Make time for God in your life. Don't steal his time.

When you converse ask God to keep the enemy away and to help you hear him clearer. Start reading Scripture and ask him to give you verses for confirmation.

Do not stop pursuing him!

WAIT!

Do you like to wait? Is waiting in line fun? Or waiting on hold for what seems like hours? For most people waiting seems unnatural. But to the passionate believer who pursues God, waiting is exciting.

They long to wait for him.

Like most things in life, waiting is an exercise; it is a discipline that must be learned over time. Don't get discouraged if you don't hear right away. God wants your attention; not necessarily your sacrificial presence.

Don't give up!

Waiting is an integral part of getting to know God, but there is more. As mentioned earlier, being aware of God is foundational and coupled with waiting you will soon have a dynamic relationship with him.

Wouldn't it be wonderful for God to speak to you to:

- Hear him tell you what car to choose?
- Know what person to date?
- Know the right words to say to someone?
- Know what house to buy?

- Know what it's like to love God and know he loves you?

God desires an intimate relationship with you, not a long–distance pen pal.

Developing a relationship with God takes time. The more you spend time with him the stronger and clearer his voice becomes. When life gets problematic the first response some Christians have is to give up (even if it is for a moment in time) or ignore God's voice altogether.

FIRST RESPONSE

What is your first response to a difficult situation?

Do you instantly get angry when a problem arises?

If you are not stopping and listening to God, especially when a conflict arises are you any different than a Humanistic–Christian?

Your first response to situations defines your relationship with God.

Take to heart Paul's words to Titus (3:2) "…to speak evil of no one, to avoid quarreling, to be gentle, and to show perfect courtesy toward all people."

A change in lifestyle means you must consider your first response motives. When you converse with God ask him to help you with your first response. The Holy Spirit illuminates the deficiencies that are keeping you from a rich, rewarding, relationship with him. But working on a closer relationship with him sometimes means doing things that are difficult. But the outcome is a deeper, and more exciting relationship. You will begin to experience new things and understand his will much clearer.

NO FEAR

When you make plans are you including God in ALL of your activities and concerns? One of the greatest conflicts of God–included plans are the what–ifs and fear is the precursor to the *what–ifs*:

- What–if I can't pay this bill on time?
- What–if this relationship doesn't work?
- What–if I don't get the raise?
- What–if my kids get into trouble?

What–ifs and First Response both connect to your relationship with God. Is he your provider, your Jehova-Jireh (Hebrew for *Jehovah will provide*)? Is he your God?

Either you trust God to be who he is, or you don't.

What do you choose?

MY VOICE OR GOD'S VOICE

You hear God's voice clearer and clearer as you spend time with him. In the beginning, you may fail at hearing him clearly. But don't give up. This is where you can learn from Paul's Olympic athlete analogy:

- You build spiritual muscles when you are sitting alone listening.
- You build spiritual endurance when you give him your time.
- You build spiritual intimacy when you converse with him.
- You build spiritual awareness when you think of him.

The question I am asked the most is: "How do I distinguish between my voice and God's voice?" The answer is found in how serious you are about hearing his voice. Remember the weightlifting example? It won't happen overnight. Can an occasional jogger compete effectively in a marathon? Probably not.

At first, it may be uncomfortable.

It's new.

It may take a few days, a few weeks, or possibly a few months. But God is waiting for you. The more time you spend in conversation and listening with him the clearer and quicker you will hear him. My wife always says, "God is a gentleman when he speaks."

He isn't loud.

He isn't angry. If you hear a voice that is sarcastic, loud, or anything other than loving, it is not God speaking to you.

The key is to keep trying.

Don't give up!

FINAL THOUGHTS

Wouldn't it be nice if you heard God's voice and it sounded like Liam Neeson or Morgan Freeman? The fact is that God speaks to each of us in a unique, personal way. It is up to you to decide whether or not you want to discipline your lifestyle to align with God. Maybe you have tried to spend a week in quiet and feel like you haven't heard from him.

Don't give up.

Many people want the dessert like energy–charged worship services and socially acceptable sermons. But few will take the next step and experience a life–changing relationship with him.

Why?

Because it takes energy.

Work on your part to breakthrough to understand the character and will of God. Take to heart what G.K. Chesterton says about the Christian life, "Christianity has not been tried and found wanting; it has been found difficult and not tried."[1] Some give up after their salvation experience. They try to converse but find it difficult, often because they think it's

---

1 Chesterton, G.K.. 1956. *What's Wrong With The. World.* Sheed and Ward: NY

boring and God doesn't answer their prayers.

Joy Dawson has spent her lifetime researching and seeking God's character to understand and know him. She says, "The more time you spend studying God's character and ways, the easier you will recognize His precious voice."[2]

What would Christianity be like if people just gave up and disregarded the words of God directing us to know him? We wouldn't have leaders like Smith Wigglesworth, Brother Lawrence, Thomas Merton, Keith Green, and so many others that didn't give up.

Aren't you to follow Jesus' example? If he did it shouldn't you? In John (11: 41–42) Jesus says "Father, I thank you that you have heard me. I knew that you always hear me." Right after this affirmation to his Father, Jesus raises Lazarus from the dead.

Do you *know* that God hears you? You could know by experience. Great things will happen when you know that God hears. This is knowing his *character.*

As a teenager, I remember singing the old hymn

---

2 Dawson.

by Alfred Ackley, *He Lives*. The first part of the chorus proclaims:

> *"He lives, He lives,*
> *Christ Jesus lives today!*
> *He walks with me and talks with me*
> *Along life's narrow way."*

I struggled with that song because I never heard him *talk with me*. How many times do you sing a song and your words *fly up*, but you don't have a relationship with God and know that he can talk with you *along life's narrow way*? But it is an emotional song and you feel good afterward, right?

Here is a simple way to begin a deeper relationship with God, but you may have to consider re-doing your devotional time:

- First – Try spending a moment or two getting your heart ready to hear. Say something like this, "God, prepare my heart to hear you."
- Then – Take 5 minutes and read the Word.

- Next – Then converse for 5 minutes for whatever is in your heart.
- Finally – Spend 5 minutes quietly listening for his voice.

This is a great time to put into practice Centering Prayer. As you gain more endurance expand your time to ten minutes each. Then keep adding more time.

Soon you will be talking to him all day; back and forth – he speaks, you listen, you speak, he listens. It is an amazing experience when you can walk in communion with God and be prompted by the Holy Spirit.

This is *walking in the Spirit.*

If you are not willing to make changes and fully understand that having a relationship with God doesn't come overnight, then you will never be able to understand what Jesus meant when he said, "I have come that they may have life and have it to the full." (John 10:10). The KJV reads, "I am come that they might have life and that they might have it more abundantly."

Have you stopped to consider why Paul, James, Peter, and other apostles, disciples, prophets, and other early believers continued to seek a relationship with God when everything around them was falling apart? They were beaten, stoned, whipped, almost drowned, and imprisoned. Now you may thinking, "But that they were different – they were saints!"

- The only difference between them and you is their relationship with God.
- They knew God would provide fruit on the other side of their trials.
- They didn't rely on their emotions.
- They didn't focus on circumstances.
- They knew that God had a purpose – even though they couldn't see it in the natural.
- They relied on their *experiential foundation;* their *relationship with God.*

To hear God clearly you must know God intimately. You must work hard every day to draw near to him and to understand your hurts, your sin, your selfishness, and work through them so you can hear him accurately.

We all are mystic/saints.

Some of you just haven't realized it yet.

ABOUT

D.V. Adams, PhD (Theology) has spent over 20 years studying worship and learning to how integrate God into a lifestyle of worship.

He lives with his wife, Theresa in the Pacific Northwest and enjoys spoiling his ten grandchildren.

For speaking engagements
please contact D.V. at:

drdvadams@gmail.com

COMING SOON FROM
DV ADAMS

RONAN (Novel)

THE PRACTICE OF THE PRESENCE OF GOD - STUDY GUIDE FOR SMALL GROUPS

ADAMS HISTORY OF WORSHIP

God's Voice

I am amazed at the clarity of the Scripture regarding God's voice. It is so clear that he desires to have a relationship with us, yet we rationalize his voice through pastors, evangelists, friends, and other means of communication. This is not to say that he is unable to speak to us through others, but if we would stop and look at what history has to say about God speaking to us, it is obvious that he is trying to get our attention.

The following verses is not an exhaustive list pertaining to God's voice, but a few of my favorite verses. I hope you enjoy them too.

OLD TESTAMENT

Exodus 19:19

Moses spoke, and the voice of God answered him.

Exodus 20:22

Then the Lord said to Moses, "Tell the Israelites this: 'You have seen for yourselves that I have spoken to you from heaven...'"

Deuteronomy 30:20

...and that you may love the LORD your God, listen to his voice, and hold fast to him.

1 Kings 19:12

After the earthquake came a fire, but the Lord was not in the fire. And after the fire came a gentle whisper.

1 Samuel 15:22 (ESV)

And Samuel said, "Has the Lord as great delight in burnt offerings and sacrifices, as in obeying the voice of the Lord? Behold, to obey is better than sacrifice, and to listen than the fat of rams."

2 Samuel 22:14

The LORD thundered from heaven; the voice of the Most High resounded.

Psalm 29:4

The voice of the Lord is powerful; the voice of the Lord is majestic.

Psalm 34:1
Come, you children, listen to me; I will teach you the fear of the LORD.

Psalm 81:8

Hear me, my people, and I will warn you— if you would only listen to me, Israel!

Psalm 95:6-8

Come, let us bow down in worship, let us kneel before the

Lord our Maker for he is our God and we are the people of his

pasture, the flock under his care. Today, if only you would hear

his voice, do not harden your hearts.

Proverbs 7:4

Now therefore, my sons, listen to me, And pay attention to the

words of my mouth.

Isaiah 6:8

Then I heard the voice of the Lord saying, Whom, shall I send?

And who will go for us? And I said, "Here am I. Send me!"

Isaiah 28:23

Listen and hear my voice; pay attention and hear what I say.

Isaiah 30:21

Whether you turn to the right or to the left, your ears will hear a

voice behind you, saying, "This is the way; walk in it."

Micah 1:2

Hear, you peoples, all of you, listen, earth and all who live in it, that the Sovereign LORD may bear witness against you, the Lord from his holy temple.

Malachi 2:2

"If you do not listen, and if you do not take it to heart to give honor to My name," says the LORD of hosts, "then I will send the curse upon you and I will curse your blessings; and indeed, I have cursed them already, because you are not taking it to heart."

NEW TESTAMENT

Matthew 17:5

While he was still speaking, a bright cloud covered them, and a voice from the cloud said, "This is my Son, whom I love; with him I am well pleased. Listen to him!"

John 3:29

The bride belongs to the bridegroom. The friend who attends the bridegroom waits and listens for him and is full of joy when he hears the bridegroom's voice.

John 8:47

Whoever belongs to God hears what God says. The reason you do not hear is that you do not belong to God.

John 10:8

All who came before Me are thieves and robbers, but the sheep did not hear them.

John 10:27

My sheep listen to my voice; I know them, and they follow me.

John 11: 41-42

Father, I thank you that you have heard me. I knew that you always hear me.

Hebrews 3:15

As has just been said: 'Today, if you hear his voice, do not harden your hearts as you did in the rebellion.'

Revelation 3:20

Here I am! I stand at the door and knock. If anyone hears my voice and opens the door, I will come in and eat with him, and he with me.

BIBLIOGRAPHY
(and other great reads)

à Kempis, Thomas. 1952. *The Inner Life*. Penguin Books: NY

Avila, Teresa. 1991. *The Way of Perfection*. Doubleday: NY

Becker, Margaret. 2006. *Coming Up for Air: Simple Acts to Redefine Your Life*. NavPress: CO

Brother Lawrence. 1982. *The Practice of The Presence of God*. Whitaker House: Springdale, PA

Brown, Tom. 1978. *The Tracker*. Berkley Books: NJ

Bucholz, Ester. 1997. *The call of solitude; How spending time alone can enhance intimacy*. Simon and Schuster: NY. Psychology Today. Publication Date: Jan/Feb 1998

Burger, J.M. 1995. *Individual Differences in Preferences For Solitude*. Journal of Research in Personality. 29, 85-108

Chambers, Oswald. 2010. *My Utmost For His Highest.* Discovery Books: Grand Rapids, MI

Chesterton, G.K.. 1956. *What's Wrong With The World.* Sheed and Ward: NY

Dawson, Joy. 2006. *Forever Ruined for the Ordinary: The Adventure of Hearing and Obeying God's Voice.* YWAM Publishing: Edmonds, WA

Dessen, Sarah. 2008. *Just Listen.* Speak: NY

Foster, Richard. 1978. *Celebration of Discipline.* Harper: San Francisco 1992. *Prayer: Finding The True Hearts Home.*

Gardner, E'yen A. 2010. *Humbly Submitting to Change - The Wilderness Experience.* Printed Word Publishing.

Gibran, Kahlil. 1923. *The Prophet.* Alfred A. Knopf: NY

Hallowell, Edward. 2006. *Crazybusy.* Ballantine Books: NY

Hanh, Thich Nhat. 1995. *Living Buddha, Living Christ.*
  Riverhead Books: NY

Keating, Thomas. 2006. *Open Mind, Open Heart.*
  Bloomsbury Academic: London

Kundtz, David. 1998. *Stopping: How To Be Still When You
  Have To Keep Going.* Conari Press: Berkeley, CA

Laubauch, Frank. 2012. *The Game With Minutes.*
  Martino Fine Books: Eastford, CT
                    2007. *Letters by a Modern Mystic:
                    Excerpts from Letters Written at Dansalan,
                    Lake Lanao, Philippine Islands, to His
                    Father.*

Lewis, C.S. 1949. *The Weight of Glory: And Other Addresses.*
  HarperCollins: NY

Tomlinson, Mack. 2010. *In Light of Eternity, The Life of Leonard Ravenhill.* Free Grace Press: Conway, AR

Wigglesworth, Smith. 2000. *Greater Works: Experiencing God's Power.* Whitaker House: New Kensington, PA

Willard, Dallas. 1991. *The Spirit of Disciplines:Understanding How God Changes Lives.* Harper: San Francisco

Young, Wm. Paul. 2012. *Crossroads.* Hatchette Book Group: NY

CPSIA information can be obtained
at www.ICGtesting.com
Printed in the USA
FSHW011905180819
61170FS